The Celtic Cross

Studies in Irish Culture and Literature

The Celtic Cross

Studies in Irish Culture and Literature

edited by
Ray B. Browne
William John Roscelli
and
Richard Loftus

Essay Index Reprint Series

BOOKS FOR LIBRARIES PRESS
FREEPORT, NEW YORK

The day is not—the day was never near—
   Could desolate
The Destined Island, all whose clay
   Is holy ground.
                    From "The Celtic Cross" by
                    Thomas D'Arcy McGee
                    (1825-68)

INTERNATIONAL STANDARD BOOK NUMBER:
0-8369-1744-8

LIBRARY OF CONGRESS CATALOG CARD NUMBER:
78-121453

PRINTED IN THE UNITED STATES OF AMERICA

Preface

The papers in this volume, with two exceptions, were read at the first conference of the American Committee for Irish Studies, held at Purdue University in 1963. Although the papers were commissioned, each author was left free to develop his topic according to his own inclinations. The result is a diverse collection which provides a variety of perspectives in the study of Ireland and its culture.

The papers are published here in cooperation with the American Committee for Irish Studies. Prof. Lawrence J. McCaffrey of Marquette University, secretary of the ACIS, edited the papers of Emmet Larkin and Gilbert Cahill and made other editorial contributions to the volume. The remaining papers were jointly edited by Ray Browne and William Roscelli. Richard Loftus represented the ACIS.

In preparing the manuscripts for publication, the editors have occasionally made minor alterations in passages originally designed more for the ear than for the eye, and have deleted a few informal comments delivered in the relaxed atmosphere generally prevailing at the conference. But in no instance has the integrity of any paper been violated.

We are especially grateful to Austin Clarke for permission to quote extensively from his *Later Poems*.

The Editors

Contents

LITERATURE

James Joyce and Austin Clarke had certain experiences in common. Both attended Belvedere College and owed their education to the Jesuits. Both endured an adolescent conflict between sex and religion. Both had trouble with the Church. Both suffered anguish unrelieved by proper guidance. For both, this conflict between flesh and spirit left a wound in the soul. In this sense, Joyce and Clarke belong together: Ireland was their provocation. It takes only a slight adaptation to make Auden's dictum on Yeats apply to them: "Mad Ireland hurt them into poetry."

On the other hand, Joyce's name is the proverbial household word among the literate, but Clarke's is known only to students of modern Irish literature and to readers of the Saturday book page of the Irish Times, where his poetry and reviews have appeared. Portrait of the Artist is required reading in nearly all English-speaking colleges. The impulse to explicate Joyce continues because there is so much for it to feed on.

Clarke's poetry deals with the personal and public aspects of the problem of religion. The personal problem is that the comforting religious faith of his youth has been destroyed by experience, disillusion, and the appeal of intellect and art. "The

9

Straying Student" is a good example of his conflict between religion and art. The public aspect of the conflict is posed by the problems of religion in modern Ireland. In "Burial of an Irish President," for instance, Clarke is bothered by the fact that at Douglas Hyde's funeral, the Catholic members of the Irish Cabinet did not attend the Protestant services at St. Patrick's.

The three essays on Clarke included in this collection constitute a deep and scholarly critique of the man and his poetry.

J. C. Lehane

Stephen's Aesthetic in
A Portrait of the Artist

Edward Brandabur

The aesthetic theory in James Joyce's *A Portrait of the Artist* has probably elicited more critical response than the novel itself. Instead of considering the theory as integral to the dramatic context of the novel, most critics have studied it in isolation, as if Joyce had meant the Stephen-Lynch dialogue mainly for instruction. Two main views derive from this concern with the isolated theory. Critics such as Harry Levin,[1] Maurice Beebe,[2] and Haskell Block,[3] have examined the theory in terms of its historical-philosophical connections and decided, contrary to Stephen's assertion, that the theory is more Pateresque than Thomistic: others, like J. Mitchell Morse, maintain the theory to be, indeed, "applied Aquinas."[4] Father William Noon has shown Stephen's inadequate comprehension of St. Thomas; Shiv Kumar has suggested a relationship between Stephen's aesthetic and that of Bergson.[5] Touched by the "New Criticism," Hugh Kenner[6] and Walton Litz[7] have looked on the aesthetic theory as a key to Joyce's aesthetic practice from *Dubliners* to *Finnegans Wake*.

Though enlightening, these approaches do not sufficiently explain the role of Stephen's aesthetic theory. The novel should be taken first as a "portrait of the artist," and therefore one rightly expects everything in the novel to render the "quidditas" of Stephen: the dialogue with Lynch serves this intention. The aesthetic theory provides a quasi-solution to certain complex personal problems which Stephen could not have solved in the environment Joyce created for him. These problems are not primarily aesthetic, nor peculiar to an artist: but their quasi-solution only an artist might devise.

In the novel the best example of the use of aesthetic theory to solve Stephen's personal malaise appears in the villanelle episode, which immediately follows Stephen's theoretic exposition. Although suggested by Grant Redford, the relationship of statement and rendering between these episodes has not been studied in detail.[8] In composing the villanelle, his homage to Emma Clery, Stephen practices what he had just expounded to Lynch, to whom he had developed three aspects of his theory: the nature of the aesthetic object, its relation to a beholder, and the character of artistic creation, of which he has said least. All three aspects incarnate during Stephen's composition of the poem, but the last is emphasized. For in the villanelle episode Joyce portrays what Stephen has defined for Lynch as the "phenomena of artistic conception, artistic gestation and artistic reproduction."[9] For these phenomena he requires "a new terminology and a new *personal experience* (475, Italics mine)." Stephen sets forth the phases of aesthetic apprehension, during which the mind perceives a thing in its *integritas, consonontia,* and *quidditas:* this last, "the supreme quality felt by the artist when the esthetic image is first conceived in the imagination (479)," a moment for which he recalls Galvani's phrase "the enchantment of the heart," and Shelley's comparison with "a fading coal." One should expect the next episode in the novel to begin with a moment in Stephen's life as artist when an aesthetic object undergoes its conception, gestation, and reproduction.

Stephen awakens to "a tremulous morning knowledge," touched by that previously mentioned "enchantment of the heart." He compares his imagination to Mary's womb, his inspiration like that of the Holy Spirit, through Whom Christ was conceived: "the instant flashed forth like a point of light and now from cloud on cloud of vague circumstance confused form was veiling softly in its afterglow. O! In the virgin womb of the imagination the word was made flesh. Gabriel the seraph had come to the virgin's chamber (484)." In these analogies, an ethereal purity proves the common factor—Stephen's artistic generation, "pure as purest water." But further, the "point of light" previously compared to the operation of God's Spirit becomes an image for Emma Clery: "An afterglow deepened within his spirit, whence the white flame had passed, deepening to a rose and ardent light. That rose and ardent light was her strange wilful heart." Unlike God's Holy Intentions, borne through the Holy Spirit, the desires attributed to Emma arise from a heart eager to seduce the angels: "lured by that ardent roselike glow the choirs of the seraphim were falling from heaven."

What appeared a somewhat precious description of the origin of a poem proves on closer look paradoxical. The pure womb of imagination in the artist is yet in Emma, though now sullied, for she is thought of as luring the seraphim with a "roselike glow," and the "glow" presumably originates also from the action of Gabriel who focused the creative light of God. The artist conceives in purity, but Emma conceives in him out of such malice as to lure the seraphim who, one notes, are compared in the second stanza of the villanelle to Stephen himself: "Your eyes have set man's heart ablaze/ And you have had your will of him./ Are you not weary of ardent ways?" The suggestions of Stephen's angelic purity, as creator, and Emma's wilful malice, as seductress, fuse in an epiphany the rays of which are the rhyme of the villanelle: "the roselike glow sent forth its rays of rhyme; ways, days, blaze, praise, raise. Its rays burned up the world: the rays from the rose that was her wilful heart (484-5)."

These contradictions should not imply that Joyce fumbled his depiction of Stephen's budding creative act: though Stephen creates "at that windless hour of dawn when madness wakes," his madness is purposeful, which can be shown by analyzing the element of fusion in this episode.

The seraphic Stephen and his temptress, Emma, emerge from the beginning of this episode as though their identities were fused: their images unite also with the other elements of the imagery. Stephen's imagination is Mary's womb; but Emma is like Mary. Stephen is a seraph: a seraph fertilizes his creative imagination—but from Emma also emanates a creative light. The Joycean urge, fulfilled in *Finnegans Wake,* here unites all things as one: Stephen equals Emma equals the angel Gabriel equals the fallen seraphim equals the Virgin Mary equals Eve, and so on.

In addition to this fusion of identities, the initial phase reveals a synesthetic fusion—usually associated with the French symbolist poets but found here and elsewhere in the novel—the confusion of the perceptions of different senses. Joyce describes Stephen's awakening to aesthetic annunciation through a mingling of touch and sight imagery: "over his limbs in sleep pale cool waves of light had passed." And shortly afterward, sight and sound images unite when the "roselike glow" of inspiration changes into "rays of rhyme." By the end of the episode, the whole villanelle flows over Stephen's brain in "liquid letters of speech," as though at once felt, seen, and heard.

Synesthesia appears also in the well-known earlier section in which, having rejected the priesthood, an enraptured Stephen beholds the girl in the surf; just before his vision, Stephen prepares for ecstatic fulfillment by a synesthetic disordering of perception: "Suddenly it seemed to [him] that he heard notes of fitful music leaping upwards a tone and downwards a diminished fourth, upwards a tone, and downwards a major third, like triple-branching flames leaping fitfully, flame after flame, out of midnight wood (424)." This synesthetic awareness peaks just before the sea-girl vision when Stephen recalls the phrase "a day of dappled seaborne clouds," after which, "The phrase and the day and the scene harmornized in a chord," and Stephen thinks in Rimbaudian terms: "Words. Was it their colours? He allowed them to glow and fade, hue after hue: sunrise gold, the russet and green of apple orchards, azure of waves, the greyfringed fleece of clouds (426)." And, the narrative voice explains here that Stephen "drew *less* pleasure from the reflection of the glowing sensible world through the prism of a language many coloured and richly storied than from the contemplation of an inner world of individual emotions mirrored perfectly in a lucid supple periodic prose."

The point here is not just to indicate the significant recurrence in a *Portrait* of the imagery of synesthesia, but to imply from this last quotation that throughout the novel Stephen's aestheticism derives from the need for expressing and resolving his emotional responses, rather than for the sake of art in itself. Thus, the fitful music suggests the unrest Stephen feels throughout the novel and resolves but on brief occasions, early through clumsy aesthetics and Night-town expeditions, and after the failure of a rigorous asceticism, by more fully developed aesthetic means, toward the end of the book. Similarly, the synesthesia in the villanelle episode and the fusion of the identities of Stephen and Emma, the seraphim, Gabriel, and so forth, express motions in Stephen to resolve the same not always sweet unrest which is the novel's pervading emotional tone. Awake forever in an unrest which he cannot quiet by ascetic means after the retreat, Stephen devises the aesthetic theory as a new means of tranquility. He needs something which will work in lieu of the failure of forbidden indulgence and unbearable asceticism.

The erotic character of Stephen's unrest epiphanizes as he completes the second stanza of the villanelle: "Smoke went up from the whole earth, from the vapoury oceans, smoke of her praise. The earth was like a swinging, swaying censor, a ball of incense, an ellipsoidal ball. The rhythm died out at once; the cry of his heart was broken. His lips began to murmur the first verses over and over; he went on stumbling through half verses, stammering and baffled; then stopped. The heart's cry was broken (485)." Earlier, the ellipsoidal ball had acquired an erotic connotation on the lips of Stephen's irreverent classmate, Moynihan, who, hearing the expression in a physics lecture, had leaned towards Stephen and murmured: "What price ellipsoidal balls! Chase me, ladies, I'm in the cavalry! (455)." Stephen's reaction to Moynihan's "rude humour" had then run "like a gust through the cloister of [his] mind, shaking into gay life limp priestly vestments that hung upon the walls, setting them to sway and caper in a sabbath of misrule (455)." The recollection of rude humour once again rustles the garments in Stephen's imagination: he loses the rhythm of the villanelle and tumbles into a misrule rooted in the erotic and leading to the irascible. Therefore the second phase of the villanelle composition reveals Stephen rapidly losing aesthetic poise as he recalls scenes with Emma, at her home when she had asked him to sing; at a ball when she had danced toward him with a faint glow on her cheek, which proves the source for the "roselike glow" of aesthetic inspiration. And, most upsetting, he remembers her innocent rapport with the young priest, a recollection which so incenses him that the quiescence of artistic contemplation gives way to the most vulgar aversion: "Bah! He had done well to leave the room in disdain. . . . Rude brutal anger routed the last lingering ecstasy from his soul. It broke up violently her fair image and flung the fragments on all sides . . . distorted reflections of her image started from his memory: the flower girl in the ragged dress with damp coarse hair and a hoyden's face who had called herself his own girl . . . the kitchengirl in the next house who sang over the clatter of her plates . . . a girl who had laughed gaily to see him stumble when the iron grating in the footpath near Cork Hill had caught the broken sole of his shoe, a girl he had glanced at as she passed out of Jacob's biscuit factory (487-8)." Through a different kind of fusion of identity, Stephen's irascibility expresses itself by demeaning Emma into the fragmented images of those lower-class women by whom he has felt at least physically accepted. But, having assaulted Emma, Stephen next recognizes his anger as "also a form of homage." He remembers railing against the young priest because Emma had left Stephen to "whisper of her innocent transgressions in the latticed ear of a priest" to whom, instead of to Stephen, she would unveil her "soul's shy nakedness." He would have preferred her confessing to him, "a priest of the eternal imagination, transmuting the daily bread of experience into the radiant body of everliving life." The "radiant image of the eucharist" suddenly dispels Stephen's anger and unites again in "an instant his bitter and despairing thoughts (488)." Poised anew, Stephen initiates the final phase in his poetic composition, the quiescence of his desire for Emma by means of the static beatitude of art, about which he has theorized. Especially the sacramental aspect of his theory may be explained by this final process.

For Stephen, art is the eucharistic transubstantiation of daily experience into art: through his art here, Stephen really changes the bread of Emma's angering refusal to uncover her soul to him into something new. At the end of the villanelle episode, "in the mysterious ways of the spiritual life," Emma yields her body, if not her spirit, to Stephen: "conscious of his desire she was waking from odorous sleep, the temptress of his villanelle . . . Her nakedness yielded to him, radiant, warm, odorous and lavishlimbed, enfolded him like a shining cloud." Stephen's bitterness and despair, which had arisen from his frustration with Emma, vanish when through his artistic eucharist, he gets what he wants, even though it is a fictional gratification. Like Shem in *Finnegans Wake*, Stephen must be crucified on "the cross of his own cruel fiction:"[10] through the quasi Mass of his art Stephen dies to the flesh, transcends nature and rises purified "by the liquid letters of speech, symbols of the element of mystery," which flows over his brain at the end of this episode.

Earlier, guilt had been associated with Emma's imagined malice in luring the seraphic artist, but that guilt had been projected from Stephen, whose own remorse epiphanized at the recollection of Moynihan's remark: in the final phase, Stephen thinks of himself as having wronged an innocent Emma: "He began to feel that he had wronged her. A sense of her innocence moved him almost to pity her, an innocence he had never understood till he had come to the knowledge of it through sin, an innocence which she too had not understood while she was innocent or before that strange humiliation of her nature had first come upon her, then first her soul had begun to live as his soul when he had first sinned (490)." Stephen had felt remorse vehemently early in the novel when, before the retreat, during the period of orgiastic riot, he had pondered darkly "the evil seed" of his lust breeding the other deadly sins as well. In adolescent self-loathing he had recoiled into an extreme and futile asceticism after the retreat: he had never stopped seeking such an exaltation of his spirit that he could regard himself seraphically pure. He had come to realize the impossibility of living as an angel, without sensual gratification. He threw over the Church for its seeming to require real angelism of him, but he retained the need to be an angel along with the need to be sensual. Only in fiction can such contradictory aspirations live together. In the last phase of the villanelle episode, Stephen is both enfolded by his lavish-limbed Emma, and purified by the same liquid letters of speech, of which his erotic phantasy is concocted.

Briefly to restate the internal structure of the villanelle episode: the instant of aesthetic conception in Stephen, and the instant at which his desire for Emma is aroused are one: unaware of the erotic character of his art, Stephen recalls Moynihan's irreverent remark. This gross epiphany briefly shatters his equanimity, so that in the second phase he turns away from the object of desire and demeans Emma. The radiant eucharistic image signifies the sacramental character of his art and leads into the final stage of his creation in which desire, once again aroused, comes to rest in a "luminous silent stasis of esthetic pleasure (479)." In the creative tabernacle, poetry transubstantiates the bread of unsatisfiable desires and purifies them through the sacrament of art.

One looks back through the novel to find that the question of how to be an artist in an alien environment is a peripheral concern for Stephen. His main problem is personal and moral, prosaic even. Stephen really wants to achieve identity through personal relationships, especially with that ideal woman who would satisfy his precocious erotic and psychic drives, and the nets in his own spirit and in Ireland prevent him. This problem, developed and intensified throughout the novel, is the one persisting concern of Stephen once it has arisen, and the novel deals with a series of attempts to solve it. Stephen's choice of the way of Dedalus shows that, finally, nothing solves his problem but escape from it.

In such a context, the novel moves from Stephen's childhood apprehension of Eileen to his final exodus, still unsatisfied in his quest. The images which bridge his early desire and the final as yet uncreated object of his search are the "long thin cool white hands of Eileen," and the "white arms of road," with their "promise of close embraces" on the last page of the book. By falling into the white arms of the world Stephen shall imagine his union in the "real world" with what he thinks of early in the novel while brooding on his Mercedes: "the unsubstantial image which his soul so constantly beheld (311)." That he ultimately chooses not a determinate goal but a road suggests the final irony of *A Portrait of the Artist:* we see Stephen finally much as we recall the young boy in Joyce's "Araby," which is a clearer commentary on the romantic quest for the elusive because illusory object: the young boy saw himself "a creature driven and derided by vanity."[11]

The quest for the "unsubstantial image" progresses in several stages of which the composition of the villanelle in some ways is an unsatisfactory culmination. In the first phase, after his childish attraction for Eileen, Stephen imagines himself as the Count of Monte Cristo, free now for a liaison with Mercedes: but, posturing in phantasy as the romantic hero, Stephen rejects a relationship with even an imaginary Mercedes. He imagines "standing in a moonlit garden with a Mercedes who had so many years before slighted his love, and with a sadly proud gesture of refusal, saying: Madam, I never eat muscatel grapes (308-9)."

Nevertheless, Stephen's adolescent posturing stems from the unrest which prods him into the more determinate posture of the artist. He imagines his "strange unrest" culminating in a moment of romantic transfiguration when "he would fade into something impalpable and . . . in a moment . . . be transfigured (311)." The opportunity for transfiguration comes shortly after his period of romantic imagining. Stephen tries to hide from others the now feverish unrest "of his blood" excited at a children's party by the sight of Emma Clery; and shortly afterward in a now *real* gesture of refusal he fails to catch hold of her as they ride home on the tram. "He heard what her eyes said to him from beneath their cowl and knew that in some dim past, whether in life or revery, he had heard their tale before . . . a voice within him spoke . . . asking him would he take her gift . . . [but] he stood listlessly in his place, seemingly a tranquil watcher of the scene before him (316)."

From this point on, Stephen remains for the most part "a tranquil watcher of the scene before him"; and he reserves for his imagination the union with Emma, with whom, until the end of the novel, he will be more constantly preoccupied than with any other thought or image. His gesture of refusal leads to a precocious and awkward attempt at poetry, dedicated to Emma, as he will later write the villanelle in her honor. The tram episode and subsequent poem parallel Stephen's later imagined rejection by Emma and the consequent villanelle; so that the connection between Stephen's desire for union with an unsubstantial image of woman and his artistic creation appears here in embryonic form. Stephen does not permit the real resolution of his desire for Emma, for on the tram steps he avoids catching hold of her as one would expect: rather, on the next day the fulfillment of his desire is a poem, the verses of which "told . . . of some undefined sorrow . . . hidden in the hearts of the protagonists . . . and when the moment of farewell had come the kiss which had been withheld by one was given by both (317-18)." Aroused in reality, the desire is achieved through art.

Contrary to Harry Levin's assertion that the heroine has been "refined out of existence" in *A Portrait*,[12] Emma comes closer than any woman to being Stephen's unsubstantial image incarnate, and therefore her influence on him has been unjustly slighted. Had she actually corresponded to the image, Stephen's choice at the end of the novel might have been different. After a chance encounter with Emma, Stephen wavers in his resolve to leave Ireland: "Yes, I liked her today. A little or much? Don't know. I liked her and it seems a new feeling to me. Then, in that case, all the rest, all that I thought I thought and all that I felt I felt, all the rest before now in fact . . . O, give it up, old chap! Sleep it off (524-5)." He finally chooses flight, but even this, as his posture in *Ulysses* shows, is not adequate.

Stephen broods frequently on Emma. His first poem is about her. He thinks only of his appearance in her eyes during the Whitsuntide play. During the turmoil of the retreat he thinks of her, and, with the sigh of relief as he is about to be shriven, comes the feeling that the way is now clear for an innocent relationship between himself and Emma. During the exposition of aesthetic theory, to which Stephen adheres in spite of Lynch's derogation and Dononan's arrogance, Stephen is finally distracted and prepared for the villanelle episode by Lynch's remark on seeing Emma: "Your beloved is here." Stephen feels at once "a conscious bitterness"; his mind empties "of theory and courage," and lapses "back into a listless peace (482)," a mood similar to his earlier description as "a tranquil watcher of the scene before him (316)." From this mood, it is a step to the "luminous silent stasis of aesthetic pleasure" that comes to be the resolution of his desire.

From the other women in his life, Stephen had derived fragments of the unsubstantial image: his mother, Eileen, and Mercedes early bring out the desire in him: the prostitute who initiates him into the physical life but briefly appeases, and the surf-girl calls forth an ecstasy intense but ephemeral. In Emma most of these fragments unite, but even she dissatisfies. Insufficient of soul, she cannot be a soul-mate. In *Stephen Hero*, the budding artist had striven to discover in Emma something "worthy of so significant a name as soul . . . but he could not."[13]

Although not stressed in *A Portrait*, Emma's marsupiality obliges Stephen to construct his own soul-mate in the eternal imagination: for this the aesthetic theory is a blueprint, art an illusory fulfillment, exile a necessary condition. Though briefly inclined to turn back to Emma and life in Ireland, Stephen writes in his journal: "I opened the spiritual-heroic refrigerating apparatus, invented and patented in all countries by Dante (524)." I take this to mean that role of poet-hero is for Stephen as much a mode of anesthesia as a way of coming alive through artistic self-expression, despite the rhetorical effect of the book.

In his essay on Keats' "Ode on a Grecian Urn," Cleanth Brooks justifies the poem's final lines on the grounds that they are intrinsic to the dramatic context of the whole poem. They can be understood only in that context, so that to deal with them in isolation amounts to critical injustice. My view of the role of the aesthetic theory in *A Portrait* is that of Brooks toward the utterance of Keats' "Urn." But I do not think, as Brooks does of the Ode, that *A Portrait of the Artist* is a work of paradox, which suggests that what appears irreconcilable is only apparently so. Stephen chooses to fictionalize life, through art, by way of getting what he feels denied in life. He chooses neither perfection of the life nor the work: he chooses stasis, the only medium of contradiction. Because it lacks a valid resolution of the central problem dealt with, the novel suffers as a work of art. But, perhaps, after all, it is Joyce's subtle irony toward Stephen which redeems the book.

Notes

1 *James Joyce* (Norfolk, Conn.: New Directions, 1941).

2 "Joyce and Aquinas: The Theory of Aesthetics," *Philological Quarterly*, XXXVI (January, 1957), 20-35.

3 "The Critical Theory of James Joyce," *Journal of Aesthetic and Art Criticism*, VIII (March, 1950), 172-84.

4 *The Sympathetic Alien* (New York: New York University Press, 1859).

5 *Joyce and Aquinas* (New Haven: Yale, 1957); "Bergson and Stephen Dedalus' Aesthetic Theory," *Journal of Aesthetic and Art Criticism*, XVI (Sept., 1957), 124-27.

6 *Dublin's Joyce* (Bloomington: Indiana University Press, 1956).

7 *The Art of James Joyce* (New York: Oxford University Press, 1961).

8 "The Role of Structure in Joyce's 'Portrait,'" *Modern Fiction Studies* (Spring, 1958), pp. 21-30. Wayne Booth seems about to consider the villanelle episode in detail, but beyond asking questions about the quality of the villanelle itself (questions which he does not answer), he does not fulfill the reader's expectations for an explication of this difficult section. *The Rhetoric of Fiction* (Chicago: University of Chicago Press, 1961), pp. 328-30.

9 This and subsequent references to *A Portrait of the Artist as a Young Man* are from *The Portable James Joyce*, ed. Harry Levin (New York: Viking Press, 1959).

10 New York: Viking Press, 1959, p. 192.

11 In *The Portable James Joyce*, p. 46.

12 *James Joyce*, p. 47.

13 Ed. Theodore Spencer. Revised edition with additional material by John J. Slocum and Herbert Cahoon (London: Jonathan Cape, 1956).

Comment

Maurice Beebe

Many readers think that Stephen's theory of aesthetics is a kind of excrescence upon Joyce's *Portrait of the Artist,* an abnormal growth that has no dramatic relationship to the story of Stephen's development. For me, therefore, the main importance of Edward Brandabur's challenging essay is its demonstration that the aesthetic theory is indeed functional, that it is closely related to the major themes of the novel, and that it tells us as much about the psychology of Stephen as about the nature of art. We may go a step further, perhaps, and say that the theory of aesthetics performs much the same function in the *Portrait* as the sermon at the retreat. No one would deny that Stephen is profoundly altered by hearing the sermon, and if he is changed too after he formulates his contrasting religion of art and delivers *his* sermon on the subject, then these two essays-within-a-novel are meant to balance each other. I am in full agreement with what I take to be Brandabur's central thesis.

Nonetheless, I would not be doing my duty here if I were not prepared to quibble over a few points. Brandabur concludes his paper with this statement: "Because it lacks a valid resolution of the central problem dealt with, the novel suffers as a work of art. But, perhaps, after all, it is Joyce's subtle irony toward Stephen which redeems the book." I am not sure I know just what Brandabur means by "Joyce's subtle irony toward Stephen" —and I may be doing him an injustice—but the usual inference of those interpretations which emphasize irony in the *Portrait* is that Stephen is not to be taken very seriously as a true artist. In saying that "how to be an artist . . . is a peripheral concern for Stephen. His main problem is personal and moral, prosaic even," Brandabur would seem to be following the anti-Stephen view to some extent.

I will concede that there are ironic, satiric touches in Joyce's portrayal of Stephen, but it is no longer possible, I think, to accept the argument—most forcefully presented by Hugh Kenner —that the *Portrait* presents not a genuine artist, but a faker, a poser, a dilettante very different from Joyce himself. Richard

Ellmann's researches and the abundance of primary-source materials made available to us in the past decade force us to admit that Stephen is clearly based upon Joyce himself. The detachment and balance so evident in the novel we could expect in any of us looking back on the embarrassments of youth. And if we look closely enough and intently enough at any work of literature, even an *Uncle Tom's Cabin*, it may well begin to seem intentionally ironic. But when we try to establish the degree of irony in an autobiographical novel of the *Bildungsroman* sort, there is a simple test that can be applied. The hero in such books does not find his true self or his proper vocation until near the conclusion; almost always he undergoes a transformation which makes him reject the standards of his past. In Stephen's case, the transformation occurs when, having tested the claims of family, country, love, friendship, and religion, he finally learns the significance of his name and becomes the detached artist in that romantic moment of consecration when he observes, in a mood of utter stasis, the young girl wading in the stream: "His soul," we are told, "had arisen from the grave of boyhood, spurning her graveclothes." If Stephen is the fake artist, then irony should be apparent after his consecration. Most of Hugh Kenner's examples of irony are taken from the earlier pages of the novel, and having thereby established to his own satisfaction that Stephen could hardly develop into much of an artist, he finds it easy to dismiss the post-theory poem composed by Stephen. In fact, he goes further than Brandabur, for he sees the poem as the result of a wet-dream. If this is the best Stephen can do, Kenner implies, then he is still far from being the Joyce who wrote *Ulysses.*

But the point is that the Stephen depicted in the novel is, of course, no more the mature Joyce than Joyce was at the equivalent time of his life. Until at least the day after that day memorialized in *Ulysses,* Joyce—hence Stephen—had not discovered that partial compact with life which enables him to acknowledge the coexistence of two selves and to find that it is possible in life (not, as Brandabur says, only in fiction) to be both "an angel and a sensuous man." We know that Joyce discovered this partial compact through his union with Nora Barnacle, and that he knew the solution at the time he was writing the *Portrait,* though not at the time depicted.

I think that Brandabur is correct in pointing out that the theory of aesthetics has too often been seen in isolation from the novel in which it appears, but I wonder if he is not perhaps seeing the *Portrait* too much in isolation from Joyce's other works, for we know now that all of Joyce's books are closely related thematically. If, using hindsight, we look back on those passages describing Stephen's composition of the villanelle (and I agree with Brandabur that these are among the most crucial passages in the novel), we may see that Joyce is already suggesting a resolution of Stephen's central problem, which, as I see it, is how to combine art with life, exile with experience.

When Stephen talks about the three stages of artistic apprehension, the last is the recognition of radiance, *quidditas*, the peculiar whatness of the object. But whereas the observer recognizes this quality last, when the work is completed and achieves its epiphany, Stephen tells us that "this supreme quality is felt by the artist when the aesthetic image is first conceived in his imagination. The mind in that mysterious instant Shelley likened beautifully to a fading coal." This reversal is, I think, very important. If we look back at the context of Shelley's image, his description of the creative process in "A Defense of Poetry," we discover that the emphasis is on the diminishing quality of inspiration: there is first that initial flash of inspiration, "the enchantment of the heart," which is gradually dispelled as the poet begins consciously to write, so that the finished poem only approaches and never entirely attains the initial ideal within the mind of the poet. After discussing the three qualities of art, coinciding with the three stages of artistic apprehension, Stephen goes on to discuss the three main forms of art—the lyrical, the epical, and the dramatic. We may rightly expect that the passages which follow, describing Stephen's composition of the villanelle, are a demonstration of his theory. The phrase "enchantment of the heart" reappears, linking Stephen's mood when he first awakens to the third quality of art, radiance or *quidditas*. But as in Shelley's description, this is but momentary, followed by an "afterglow," for the "white flame had passed, deepening to a rose and ardent light." Brandabur suggests that this episode is important chiefly because it shows Stephen in imagination attaining a fusion between the seraphic and the sensual, and the erotic basis of this creativity is, I take it, evidence of Joyce's irony toward Stephen. However, if we recognize any progression at all in this episode, we must acknowledge that Stephen proceeds from the spiritual to the physical, from "ecstasy" to "languor," from a mood of mystic inspiration to the writing of a poem on a cigarette box. The poem that Stephen writes, with its refrain, "Tell no more of enchanted days," expresses the passing of desire and romantic aspiration, and presumably it represents only the first of Stephen's three forms of art, the lyrical. What do we make of the fact that the poem is finally completed at the moment when Emma capitulates to Stephen in his imagination? Obviously that description of her yielding to him is symbolic, and it symbolizes, I think, the way in which the forces of sensuous life capitulate before the artist's ability to transmute "the daily bread of experience into the radiant body of everlasting life." Weary now of ardent ways, but not denying the sensuous basis of his mood, Stephen has finally learned how to *use* life. It is *the artist* in Stephen, not the young man, who finally possesses and consumes Emma.

The Poetry of Austin Clarke

George Brandon Saul

The poetry of Austin Clarke has often left me, critically, in a confusion mingling doubt and approval—and sometimes merely in a confusion. His early education and religious discipline as a Roman Catholic affected his creative work even more pervasively than such phases of experience usually do. According to Robert Farren, Clarke, born in 1896 to an old Dublin family, was educated at Belvedere College and underwent an experience somewhat similar to that mirrored by Joyce in his *Portrait of the Artist*. (How fortunate, then, that he was not frightened into the postures of his better-known compatriot!)

Eventually Clarke took his B.A. from University College, Dublin, where he had studied Irish under Hyde and where he succeeded his teacher Thomas MacDonagh as lecturer in English. He became also a protégé of A.E. to whom he dedicated his *Collected Poems*. Eventually he spent twelve years as critic and reviewer in London. In 1937 he returned to Ireland, settling in Templeogue, a village near Dublin. Two years later he began broadcasting from Radio Eireann and also resumed the writing of short verse plays. In 1940 he founded with Farren the Dublin Verse-Speaking Society, which turned into the Lyric Theatre Co., controlled by him,

> 'Tis the white stag, Fame, we're a-hunting;
> Bid the world's hounds come to horn!

wrote Ezra Pound in his youthful—and charming—period of lucidity; and Clarke has been represented as a hunter whom the hounds have not obliged—this despite considerable approval in the English reviews. Precisely why he has not been accorded a general recognition more nearly commensurate with his deserts may perhaps be intimated by the comment to follow, which begins with *Collected Poems,* a book which sensibly omits all early matter Clarke does not wish to be judged by.

I

Collected Poems (New York, 1936) with an introduction and conclusion of helpful but inadequate "notes" by Ernest Boyd, reprints material drawn miscellaneously from the following volumes: *The Vengeance of Fionn* (1917, though twice misdated—1911 and 1918—and written before Clarke was twenty-one, favored by an extensive review in the London *Times Literary Supplement* and quickly going into a second edition); *The Fires of Baal* and *The Sword of the West* (both 1921; the bulk of the latter wisely excluded); *The Cattledrive in Connaught and Other Poems* (1925: the volume in which Gerald Griffin—*v. Wild Geese*—senses a stylistic change toward increased realism); *The Son of Learning* (1927: Clarke's first-published play, a three-acter); *Pilgrimage* (1929: winner of the Tailteann poetry award); and *The Flame* (1930: a one-act verse play; like its dramatic predecessor, first printed in the *Dublin Magazine,* to whose editor, Seumas O'Sullivan, it is dedicated).

If dates of earliest publication of its component parts be kept in mind, it will be noticed that *Collected Poems* justifies Farren's observation that Clarke proceeded from the epically narrative piece through the dramatic lyric to lyrical drama. This progression suggests an approach.

Padraic Colum regards *"The Vengeance of Fionn"* as essentially "a prolonged song—the song of the passing of youthfulness unto unadmired age, a song that has its burthen in 'Grainne, the girlish, the free.'" To me it seems occasionally inspired prentice work. The poet has not yet mastered his "trade." He flatters the general reader by assuming too much familiarity with his subject matter. Technically, his basically five-stressed blank verse is not free from awkward accent ("And ruddy warmths many-throated acclaim") or irregularity ("'On a boar's hot fangs, I spurn, I spurn.' A raven flew")—two defects Clarke has recurrently failed to avoid. And there is much evidence (also duplicated in later work) that not only women, in Winifred Welles' phrase, "are good at growing adjectives"—adjectives here not always logically placed ("from bronze crowded shields"). So verboseness is no surprise (the work opens with a sentence eleven lines long).

Nor is the architecture satisfying. Opening with an awkward statement of invitation to Fionn and the Fianna to visit and feast with Diarmuid and Grainne, the work first carries the old story (with some free handling of legend) to the point of Diarmuid's going into the forest to hunt the boar of Beann Gulbain. Then it recalls, through Grainne's troubled brooding, what led to the lovers' flight (again with novel insertion, making Grainne's threatened reversion to Fionn, rather than *geasa*, Diarmuid's reason for acceding to elopement). Next it reviews the affair from Fionn's and Diarmuid's points of view, respectively. Finally, it concludes abruptly with the dialogue of a young man and girl, revealing only that Diarmuid has been slain by the boar and noting "poor Grainne in the sunlight / Wrinkled and ugly." (This picture hardly makes credible Fionn's passion of a day or two earlier!) Incidentally, the mention of chariots being used in the pursuit of the lovers seems an odd insertion into Fenian tradition.

Part VI of the work mingles blank verse with irregular but frequently rhymed lyrical measures. Its opening also illustrates Clarke's tendency to pile up descriptive detail to no significant purpose, and sometimes to a dilution of dramatic effect. But there are momentary compensations, as when we are told that

> Oisin
> Arose and sang of sorrow till men dreamed
> Of women that were dead;

and when Fionn reveals his bitterness over losing Grainne:

> Only her hair
> Burns arrogant across the black ravine
> Of ruinous years.

It is these sudden moments of grace that persuade one that, whatever its faults—indeed, irritations—the work is rooted in genius; and that Ernest Boyd was to some degree justified in approving its "prodigal wealth of colour and imagery . . . enchanting magic of evocation."

Clarke's second epic venture is the mistitled *"Cattledrive in Connaught*: "mistitled" because it merely introduces the great Táin, recalling the story from Maeve and Ailill's "pillow talk" to MacDara's refusal of his bull. But even in limiting himself to stage-setting, Clarke finds room for innovations, as when, anticipating its invention by perhaps two thousand years, he introduces a concertina into the excitement.

Almost everything in the *Cattledrive* is in dialogue, underscoring that tendency toward dramatic structure early evident in Clarke. Some of this dialogue, indeed, rings false, as when the angry queen gurgles bookish phrases while her riches are being gathered for comparison with her husband's: the Maeve who orders a servant to "run and gather emeralds / From fields of light" simply doesn't sound like the forthright Amazon, publicly "combing out her dandruff," who earlier asserted, I am heady / But good in siring."

All in all, the virtues of the *Cattledrive* are those natural to straightforward storytelling; the faults, those of doubtful phraseology, as in "red strapping hair," or unclearness, as in "cut down the heavy gleams / Within the woods." Nevertheless there do seem less evident here those "Yeatsian and similar influences" in coloration and imagery which Boyd found objectionable in *The Vengeance of Fionn*. Although Clarke has never rid himself wholly (how could he?) of the consciousness of Yeats' example, his verse—except in such unimportant early pieces as those of *The Sword of the West*—suggests technical and intellectual consonance more frequently than imitation.

The third long nondramatic narrative of *Collected Poems* here to be remarked (though second in order of earliest publication) is "The Fires of Baal," which deals with Moses' farewell to his people and his ascent ("feeling in the far air / The eyes of unseen eagles watching him") into Mount Nebo.

Perhaps the trouble with this uneven, somewhat lush piece of blank verse is that Clarke, like Moses, is "Clouded / By vision" and consequently lured variously into abandoned luxuriating in language, extreme compression, or a species of private reference familiar today in poets who have to conceal their essential poverty of content. Love of color—and adjectives!—produces subordinate clauses to complicate sentences of unnatural conversation over twenty-five lines in length, permits phrases like "pampered damask," recalls half-dead nouns like *plat,* and proposes such strained concepts as that of "uncomplaining cows / Tethered by trickling milk." But on the other hand, compression can become almost Meredithian, as in "The ram still feeds the dreadful horn that locks / The gate of smaller cities"; while "private reference" appears in "A lake shore/Where thirst has cracked the earthen cylinder/That boasts a tyrant" and bits—such as "colonnades, disking with several hold,/The trade of Ophir"— which seem to force language into impossible effort. In the end, one settles for fragmentary beauties—"the sands/That sighed around his feet"; the ravines "Where the red cliffs of rhododendron are/A lasting sunset."

"The Music-Healers," another lengthy verse-narrative, revised from a piece in *The Sword of the West* and concerned with "the events preceding" the hero Cuchullin's death as suggested by an unnamed seventeenth-century manuscript, is the sort of thing which assumes far too much knowledge on the part of the reader, as Clarke's work often does. Resultant lack of clarity, with overindulgence in the assonance and internal rhyme common in Irish verse ("Of twigging tops and hazel ways where sunlight stays"), overbalances the occasional grace suggested by "the early cuckoo calling/From the green brink of May" and the epic accent achieved when the sick hero mutters, "I hear/Old thunder rutting in his Atlantic cave." But there is one remark of dreadful pertinence: "Man may destroy all things but war."

II

Of the shorter pieces, the fragmentary inclusions in "Gods and Men" (three from *The Sword of the West*) are least impressive—and re-emphasize Clarke's tendency to protract his verse sentences unreasonably through uncritical yielding to casual reference and the descriptive impulse. Thus, "Concobar in Uladh," after opening with a five-word statement, proceeds with a second sentence of twenty-three lines and a third of twenty-seven. Nor is clarity a primary characteristic; as with *The Vengeance of Fionn* and *The Cattledrive* the uninformed reader must find much of this matter confusing. Who among these could guess all that is implied of Ness's bride-gift and its consequences in the lines

> her wine-hot flesh had stayed
> The love-sick Fergus with a woman's guile,
> Unkingdomed him and throned her stripling?

And who is properly illuminated when the last line, "So rose at length the great war in the north," is sprung without any reference to the Dierdre story and the real reason why Fergus and a host (not merely "a score broken horsemen") defected to Medb?

The six pieces of *The Country of Two Mists*, confusingly mythological in background, have many felicitous comparisons and phrases: "water green as rye"; "And her voice coming softly over the meadow/Was the mist becoming rain"; "water/Where moonlight was mooring." But, despite some explanatory notes, they can be only a disturbing beauty to most readers.

The finest lyrics may be the twenty-five of "Past and Present" and "Pilgrimage." The former section contains some matter obviously restated from the Irish; both sections contain some of Clarke's most exciting pieces. The Yeatsian rumination—"Perfection of the life, or of the work"—has perhaps a corollary reflection in "No Recompense"; and there is frankness in Clarke's confession that he is "a pious poet." (In the sense of susceptibility to wonder and ecstasy, of course, all poets are pious.) But best of all, these brevities somehow suggest spaciousness, and panorama is implied even where the concentration is on small scenes; a wild air blows through them. "Pilgrimage" proper, with the author as usual concerned with "the sins/Whose hunger is the mind," is technically interesting for the high degree of success with which assonance has been cultivated (though not to the complete exclusion of perfect rhyme), intellectually inviting for what Colum has recognized as Clarke's identification of himself "with the Gaelic poets of the seventeenth and early eighteenth centuries," and aesthetically appealing for the half-visionary charm of certain items—not least marked in the grave music of "The Confession of Queen Gormlai":

> . . . my mind is stirred,
> Remembering the books
> I closed, for I am Gormlai
> And she was beautiful.

—The simple words are as moving as the equally simple ones of Stephens' lyric Deirdre.

Of the early plays The Son of Learning, appropriately dedicated to George Moore, is a three-act comedy freely elaborated from elements of the latter portion of the twelfth-century Vision of Mac Con Glinne. Neatly constructed, lively of pace, the piece does not lose from prior knowledge of source, though its implications demand even more of the reader (as in the Red Beggar's exclamation "A little ewe between two rams!"). The Flame, in contrast, is a gentle, beautiful play in irregular, but conversationally effective, blank verse. This one-act piece—concerned with how the holy flame of St. Brigid, at Kildare, all but went out when a novice, recalcitrant after dreaming of the world, brought a moment of fear and doubt to the Sisters—is on every score a moving justification of Colum's feeling that the "Irish-Romanesque world"—"the mid-Ireland, the Ireland between legend and modern history, is for Austin Clarke the country native to his mind."

III

The bulk of Clarke's published work since Collected Poems and the prose romance The Bright Temptation (1932) has consisted of verse plays and prose fiction. The little collection of lyrics, Night and Morning, issued in limited edition in 1938, contains only twelve pieces; and one of these—"No Recompense" —is reprinted from Collected Poems. And subsequent poems are relatively few.

Night and Morning is a difficult book, especially to one nurtured on Austin Dobson's belief that "Song should sing"; and the prevailing concern with assonance does not persuade me to share Colum's approval of Clarke's "new pattern," even when the rhythms are as suggestive of "public speech" as those of the later Yeats. The title piece seems an enigma of "the tormented soul"; and what lines like "The forks of heaven and this earth/ Had met, town-walled, in mortal view" mean, I wouldn't know. The whole book is opaque with an intellectualism that seems to be seeking difficult images and contorted statement (always a sign of the lesser poet), with results sometimes puzzling to the point of bafflement. Ultimate concerns go back, as tediously often in Clarke, to the fears and broodings which in medieval times found expression in things like the *Dialogus inter Corpus et Animam,* with defiant asides such as the goliardi broke tension with. Hence the preoccupation with the "Darkness that man must dread at last," perturbed by the fact that "An open mind disturbs the soul." Hence, too, the imagery curiously suggestive of the merging of the sensual and the religious ("O then the soul / Makes bold in the arms of sound"). Hence also "Knuckle and knee are all we know/When the mind is half despairing," and

No story handed down in Connaught
Can cheat a man, nor any learning
Keep the fire in, turn his folly
From thinking of that book in Heaven.

Hence, finally, the concern that "Every thought at last/Must stand in its own light."

When the poet's voice becomes muted to simple emotional statement, however, it does develop a warm timbre; and as fetching as anything in this collection seems "The Straying Student"—of a lad won from his faith by the visionary fatal woman so challenging to youthful morbidity: one whose mockery and sensuality made his mind "Bold as light in Greece," but also left him fearful that she might leave him

. . . in this land, where every woman's son
Must carry his own coffin and believe,
In dread, all that the clergy teach the young.

—One almost fancies a disturbed Oisin rousing in the shadows to protest Patric's God anew!

The verse plays following *Collected Poems* are a curious assortment. *The Viscount of Blarney and Other Plays* (1944) assembles three. The title piece, a one-acter concerned with an orphan girl's eluding the Viscount (really the devil—"father of lies"), though neat and swift in action, is not precisely a model of clarity. "The Kiss/A Light Comedy in One Act after the

French of Théodore de Banville" is a delightful playlet in which
Uirgeal, spelled into age, manipulates Pierrot into breaking the
spell by kissing her, though in the end she leaves him. This is
pure froth. Most moving is "The Plot Is Ready/A Play in
Four Scenes," its theme referred by Clarke to a semi-historical
Irish tale. The adulterous sixth-century Ard-ree Muriadach Mac
Erca, dying in consequence of flouting monkish efforts to get
him back "into line," may be a cloudy figure, as the abbot's assurance of his nick-of-time repentance may seem an unconvincing
gesture; but there is genuine power here—as when the king topples
into his stubbornly ordained grave or when his spirit returns
to draw his mistress into its supernatural light. And the blank
verse has accents of greatness as in the moment when Fergus,
looking on the sick king, mutters:

> This, this is the last pillow-fight all dread.
> No hand can wipe the centuries from his forehead
> Now.

Sister Eucharia/A Play in Three Scenes (1939) is dedicated
to Gordon Bottomley, whose intensely poetic dramas, neglected
today, may well be spiritual ancestors of Clarke's. This free-
verse piece, concerning a nun refused absolution by a priest
unable to comprehend the urgency of her assurance of approaching death, is a tense, almost horrifying work, not least effective
for its lay sister whose apparent hallucination leads to her tolling
the convent bell to signal the nun's passing.

Black Fast (1941) is a delightful and deftly managed piece
rooted in conjugal contention reflecting the "Seventh-century Controversy over the exact date of Easter."

The Second Kiss/A Light Comedy (1946) written in cleverly
rhymed pentameter, is, despite difference in heroines, even more
delightful than *The Kiss*, its logical predecessor. But this may
be only *de rerum natura!* Here we watch Pierrette, masquerading—
in connivance with Harlequin—as Columbine, tricking her husband
Pierrot into house and bed.

The Moment Next to Nothing (1953) (whose title gets no
reference in its dialogue: for illumination one must turn to Clarke's
other version of the story in *The Sun Dances at Easter*) is by
confession based on a portion of the medieval Irish *Fosterage of
the Houses of the Two Methers* (*v.* Lilian Duncan, *Eriu*, XI), but
for once difficulties are not referable to readers' ignorance, but
to occasionally oversubtle statement. Laid in Patric's Ireland,
this three-acter is concerned with Ceasan's effort to baptize a

renegade *ben-side* (originally a human and wife to the High King) desirous of conversion but aware that when her "other self comes back" she may, in piscatorial metaphor, "struggle wildly, break the rod." And of course this lovely pagan (who in the second scene shows, amazingly, a knowledge of Eve!) does vanish before Ceasan completes her baptism (though he thinks her drowned). It is all beautifully done, the verse alternating with prose only during the Latin lesson which concludes the first act. But there will be nothing new to Clarke's readers in either the implicit body-soul tension or Ceasan's pitiful cry:

> How, how can I repent or be forgiven
> When night is starring through my vows and changing
> Them?

One notices in this late work Clarke's continued delight in using nouns as verbs, as when Marravaun's prayers are said to have "oaked and spread themselves invisibly" or when Eithne remarks, "I must clay myself in time."

Clarke's *Later Poems* (1961) not only reprints *Pilgrimage* and *Night and Morning*, but assembles the residue of nondramatic verse postdating *Collected Poems: Ancient Lights* (1955). *Too Great a Vine* (1957: "Too great a vine, they say, can sour The best of clay"—"The Loss of Strength"), and *The Horse-Eaters* (1960). The latter material is preponderantly satiric, and subject to the usual risk of satire not charged with universality: likelihood that its concentration on the local and ephemeral will ultimately define it as sociological grist mainly. And indeed, some of the bitterest lives here already need every help Clarke's "Notes" can give.

The matter of *Ancient Lights* (all assonantal) and *Too Great a Vine* (gratefully furbished with considerable perfect rhyme— even though it lugs in so unusual a Scotticism as *curch!*) is largely religious or political in connotation:

> Fabulist, can an ill state
> Like ours, carry so great
> A Church upon its back?

But there is a fine anger in the third of "Three Poems about Children," concerned with an orphanage holocaust and the casuistry of a local bishop; there is despair at what industrialization is doing to Irish streams (one recalls *The Moon in the Yellow River*); there are touches of dry humor ("Content as a flea in a Connemara petticoat"!); there is room for a tribute to James Larkin; and there is reiteration of Clarke's disgust that love in

Ireland must be a religion-haunted fear. A little sad is the wry
admission which concludes "Return from England":

> When I had brought my wife
> And children, wave over wave,
> From exile, could I have known
> That I would sleep in England
> Still, lie awake at home?

In *The Horse-Eaters*, concern ranges from birth-control and
church lotteries to the slogan "Stop exporting horses. Start meat
factories here"; but unfortunately for Clarke, the matter of the
latter province must be measured against the lyric fury of Ralph
Hodgson on abuse of animals and destruction of birds, and this
drains it of much threat of comparative memorability. By and
large, the later Clarke is still preoccupied with a "mind too
horrible with life," contented to indulge in metrical puns and
compromises ("Hurrah for the Hippophagi/Tots echo: 'Lets
hip off a gee'"), given to verbalizing nouns and implying fragmentary multiple reference in somewhat Joycean fashion, and
so persistent in assonance that his one or two sonnets in traditional form come as shocks.

Glancing back, now, one may suggest summarily that Clarke's
poetry in metrical statement must be winnowed from a body of
material marked, on the one hand, by semi-obscurity and abuse
of oblique reference, excessive devotion to assonance (normally
only an ornament in English verse), verboseness (especially
descriptive) in narration, recurrent preoccupation with the
"drama of racial conscience" (cf. Enda's remark to Orla in *The
Sun Dances at Easter*: "There seemed to be two minds inside my
head, and the new one was always arguing and wrangling with
the other one"), noticeably uneven dramatic accomplishment,
technical irregularity in the blank verse, opaqueness and half
throttled statement in numerous lyrics; on the other, by charm in
handling natural backgrounds, re-enforcement of genuine learning, convincing recreation of medieval atmosphere, moments of
acute spiritual divination, freshness of figure, interludes of satiric
bite, sudden brief felicities and rumblings of epic thunder. God
pity this poet if ever the "new critics" discover the opportunities
he offers!

IV

Clarke's poetry and storytelling (even in dramatic concentration) are both most luminous in the prose fiction, even though
The Bright Temptation (1932) and *The Singing-Men at Cashel*

(1936) were originally banned by Irish censorship and *The Sun Dances at Easter* (1952), I understand, still is.

The first of these romances details a complicated series of adventures that befall the neophyte scholar Aidan, of the Abbey of Cluanmore, before and after it is sacked by the Danes. The excitement is intensified by Aidan's kidnapping, as a result of mistaken identity, and his subsequent love affair with Ethna, whose beauty suggests the converse of the "Amarantha" conceit ("the evening was earlier, so brightly her curls shone"). The young people's approaches to love, involving incredible restraint, in a flight among mountains, cromlechs, and caves; Aidan's capture by a gigantic bagman and his adventures among *side* in ancient Glen Bolcan; and much else precede the supernaturally guided reunion with Ethna, whose father, finding the couple have just slept naked together, plans to rush them into Confession and marriage to restore them "to Irish virtue"!

This high-spirited book has a tempo and capriciousness suggestive of James Stephens, but is girded by a personal poetry and mockery that cancel any suggestion of imitation. I am thinking of such passages as "The crowd was craning forward so eagerly to watch those wonders that every neck was longer than its swallow" and of the description of, a certain Maolruane's snoring, a bit too long for quoting.

There is wild, satiric poetry in this tale, which is in part a hymn to female beauty (for woman, of course, is "the bright temptation"), with jibes at what the clergy have done to the Irish, so that masturbation is represented as a frequent concern of the Confessional and even wives will not let their husbands see them naked! What tedium there is, is the tedium of George Moore— that of protracted approaches to climaxes that don't always occur, though of course the satiric spirit is responsible. ("... the young must be kept apart in Ireland because of Original Sin," says Clarke.) But there is much beautiful writing, its essential poetry enhanced by the author's great knowledge of the Irish countryside and its flora, and by the light set on his pen when it describes physical human beauty. Any strain on credibility is largely referable to Ethna's half-mystical guidance of her preordained lover.

The Singing-Men at Cashel (the reference is to the monks and scholars) is even more remarkable, returning us to Clarke's earlier interest in the tenth-century Queen Gormlai (not to be confused with Brian Boru's notorious "Gormlai," "Gormflaith," or "Karmala," as she is here referred to). Here, too, "bright temptations" operate, and the satirico-sardonic impulse is indulged, as when marriage is portrayed as "the humiliation of the Evil One," or when priestly married Cormac fights down his lust and sleeps with Gormlai without coition, or when Nial's divided soul is betrayed by his reference to the ancient races of Ireland who "had the proud look, the happiness of them who have never heard of Christ."

The immensity of charming detail in this romance is for those to discover who will. Enough to say here that the book is doubly concerned with the adventures of Anier Mac Conglinne, wandering Ireland as a renegade student, and the history of Gormlai, poet-daughter of the Ard-Ri: with her sterile and bewildered marriage to Cormac Mac Cuillenan of Cashel (who offensively insists on remaining virginal, is given to the fanatical self-flagellation and mortification of early Irish ascetics, and presently secures an annulment to become a priest); with her tragic and mistaken second marriage to Cormac's brutal foster-brother, Carrol of Leinster; and with her final happy union with the widowed young Nial, her stepmother's son. To point up certain passages, Clarke uses unidentified brief quotations from his own lyrics; indeed, the poem assigned by Anier (pp. 34-42) to "a pious layman in Connaught" reappears with minor changes as "Repentance" in *Night and Morning*.

This romance is convincing evidence that Clarke's poetry of color and descriptive detail can be most appropriately indulged in prose fiction, where sheer pace counts usually for less than it does in verse. Even his dramatic statement seems to gain power when unleashed in prose, as passages such as those detailing Anier's nightmare in the Cave of the Demons, or those recounting Ceallachan's vision, would argue. This is a beautifully written tale. The prose has magic—sometimes lonely magic ("A bird's flight below the bushes, was all that land tended only by the sun") It carries implications of a tremendous range of learning—in the old tales, poems, and traditions, as well as in medieval Irish history, the Church Fathers, and Roman Catholic theology. It captures natural beauty in meditative, unforced cadences, as when Clarke writes, "The summer sunlight was fording the narrow outlet where the Shannon flowed from the great lake." And the whole is in effect a poem celebrating the right and natural adoration of physical beauty and rational human love.

Anent Clarke's romantic fantasy *The Sun Dances at Easter*, it may be enough to endorse the reviewer in the *Dublin Magazine* for April-June 1953, who, after remarking on how "the poetic imagination makes a pattern of the conflict between Christian and pagan beliefs in a woman's sensual world, and elaborates the design with natural and supernatural motifs," concludes by asserting that here the "dreamlike quality . . . the floating legendary world, the intricate interplay of the lyrical, the profane and the ironic, make an enchanting book." But I still feel that while Clarke is a poet with moments only of greatness in his verse, which too often has substance without satisfying discipline, he is something better in the more furious tensions and natural felicities of his prose romances, whose protagonists, as John Buchan once remarked of *Wuthering Heights*, "belong to poetry," and whose pages are—like Yeats' poems—musical with the crying of birds.

The Later Poetry of Austin Clarke

Maurice Harmon

Austin Clarke grew up during the exciting years of pre-revolutionary Ireland. He witnessed the Easter Rising of 1916, the Anglo-Irish War, and felt the attraction of that romantic and idealistic period. Like other writers of his generation—Sean O'Faolain, Frank O'Connor, and Liam O'Flaherty—he was deeply affected by the violence, the bitterness, and the disillusion brought about by the Civil War; and he has not lived happily in the kind of Ireland that emerged from the days of youthful vision. Like theirs, his work reflects the change from romance to realism, from idealism and hope to something occasionally bordering on despair. It is a rebellion against what Frank O'Connor has called the "subjective, idealistic, romantic literature"[1] of the Irish Literary Revival.

He began in the manner of a Celtic Revival poet. His early work—*The Vengeance of Fionn* (1917), *The Fires of Baal* (1921), *The Sword of the West* (1921), and *The Cattledrive of Connaught and Other Poems* (1925)—are epic narratives showing the influence of Yeats, Samuel Ferguson, and William Larminie. They are romantic and idealistic in tone, with a lyrical, impressionistic beauty, and reveal a delicate metrical skill. Like Yeats, Clarke went back to Irish myth and saga, to the Cuchulain and Ossianic cycles. But gradually he worked out an important, personal handling of the old material. Where Yeats had formulated a dichotomy between the pagan, aristocratic past and the democratic present, Clarke presented a contrast between the Christian, medieval past and the dogmatic, Catholic present. Yeats had largely ignored the religious issues and after 1916 tended to concentrate on the Anglo-Irish middle nation of the eighteenth century in preference to the rising, unattractive middle class of his own time. With Clarke the religious question is central, for personal and national reasons, and it is closely associated with the native middle class whose rise to power is the greatest social event of recent Irish history.

Clarke's acceptance of religious problems as the material for his writing came as an understandable result of his experiences at home and at school. He was a highly sensitive child, the only boy in a family of twelve, of which three girls also survived. Home life was strict and the morality stern. He went to school at Belvedere and received most of his education from the Jesuits. In *Twice Round the Black Church* he writes, "Having been trained by the Jesuits from the age of seven, I am still unable to hold opinions with certainty and envy those who can trust in private judgment."[2] He deliberately avoids writing at length about his experiences as a boy because they closely resemble those encountered in *A Portrait of the Artist as a Young Man,* but there is much evidence in his writing of his unhappy boyhood when he knew "the dark night of the soul." His brief account of his spiritual and physical anguish during adolescence, the result of poor education and unenlightened guidance, makes pitiful reading. The conflict between church teaching and natural instinct began early in his life and was intensified with the years. It did not end with manhood, and in his twenties he was "dangerously ill in mind and body" and had to spend some time in a mental institution. His first marriage ended after two weeks. He spent many years wandering in Ireland, England, and the Continent, and his second marriage did not settle his emotional disturbance. It was inevitable that when he finally faced up to his own nature his writing would be the working out of religious problems.

His discovery of the Gaelic past was not accidental. At University College, Dublin, to which he went in 1913, he had Douglas Hyde as a teacher, a man of great natural simplicity and full of enthusiasm for the racial heritage. His influence on Clarke was decisive and lasting. "On the morning of our first term, he spoke of the aims and ideals of the language revival: we were all equal, all united in the Gaelic movement. . . . Those plain words changed me in a few seconds. The hands of our lost centuries were laid on me."[3] Hyde was the most important person he met at this time. But there was also George Sigerson, who introduced him to the subtleties of Gaelic prosody; there was Stephen MacKenna, who was enthusiastic about Gaelic poets; and there was Padraic O'Conaire, the Gaelic short-story writer, who taught him "to drink like a man." A possible career as a teacher and scholar was cut short by his first marriage. He had been appointed as lecturer in English at the University (1917-21) to succeed Thomas Mac Donagh, the poet-rebel, executed for his part in the Rising of 1916, but the appointment was not renewed when it was discovered he had been married in a registry office. He lived precariously in London as a book-reviewer and editor and returned finally to Ireland in 1932.

Since then he has lived in a Dublin suburb in relative obscurity, hidden by the great shadow of Yeats, and finding it difficult at any time to reach a wide audience because of the natural complexity of his method and material, its weight of legend and mythology, its theological implications, and its intensely personal nature. In recent years, however, he has been gaining greater recognition. The publication of *Later Poems* (1961) has made his poetry, usually published in small, semi-private editions, generally available for the first time since his *Collected Poems* (1936). The recent volume, to be followed by *Collected Plays* and *Early Poems,* contains five books of poetry—*Pilgrimage* (1929), *Night and Morning* (1938), *Ancient Lights* (1955), *Too Great A Vine* (1957), and *The Horse-Eaters* (1960)—and serves as a useful introduction to his work.

"Pilgrimage," the title and opening poem of *Later Poems,* retains the theme of flight which was dominant in the epic narratives, and introduces the world of early Christian Ireland. It is romantically reverent in its reference to Clonmacnoise, "that blessed place . . . crossed with light."[4] In the sound of clergy singing High Mass at Cashel, in the image of a "fasting crowd at prayer," in the thought of the intricate art forms of the period, in the depiction of penitential crowds at Croagh Patrick, and in the prayer of the ascetic, hermit Culdees, Clarke finds repose and peace. He moves quietly and lyrically in a muted atmosphere, finding resplendent images to describe the major religious manifestations of the medieval church.

The setting for many of the poems in this book is what he calls the Celtic-Romanesque period, which runs from the introduction of Christianity in the fifth century to the Norman invasions in the twelfth, which were accompanied by the reforming influences of the Continental Church. Toward the end of the fifth century, Ireland was temporarily cut off from Rome because of the barbaric invasions of Europe, with the result that the ecclesiastical organization set up by Patrick gave way to the pressures of the local social system and the example of the western British Church. The Celtic Church became monastic in character; Irishmen sought out secluded glens, islands, and mountainsides to build cells and devote themselves to prayer and fasting, and gradually banded together to form monastic establishments. As a result the administrative unit was not the territorial diocese but the monastic *familia* or *paruchia,* which became increasingly independent and powerful. Great monastic "cities" developed, centers of learning and culture but also of what is usually called "Celtic particularism," that is, of local variations in church tenets and rites. The best known of these native peculiarities were the Irish tonsure, which consisted of shaving the front of the head instead of the back, and the native method of computing Easter, which was in line with the method of Anatolius in the third century but not with the papal decision of Victorius (457). By the eleventh century simony and hereditary succession were common; inevitably the Cluniac reform reached the Irish monasteries, and the arrival of the Cistercians in the early twelfth century marked the end of their independence.

In his novels and plays, in particular, Clarke uses the medieval scene as a framework of reference for satirical comment on his own time. He opposes the medieval, monastic Church of masculine intellect to the centralizing, dogmatic Church of modern Ireland and seeks out a form of Christianity in which men of his complex nature and far-reaching intellect can exist within the Church. He has natural affinities with the greater intellectual liberty that was possible for the individual before the Council of Trent (1546-63). "Pilgrimage" is indicative of his attitude, although it does not express the full range of his relationship to the medieval scene. Clearly it provides him with a form of escape from the problems of his own life. But where the theme of flight in the early poems was vague and indefinite as to motivation and destination, here it is related to sexual temptation. The method is indirect but the material is personal. Thus, in "Celibacy" he uses the person of the ascetic monk persistently harassed by temptation in the form of a woman. It is a traditional story associated with many of the Irish hermits, and Clarke's treatment retains some of the humor with which the situation is now often treated in conversation. As a result the poem works in a complex manner. It dramatizes the temptation with sympathy and through the direct account of the hermit, but it also comments ironically on his story and becomes satirical of the whole situation. Clarke can view the subject as a personal one but also as one previously experienced, not unique but typical. The conjunction of past and present, impersonal and personal, absurd and exaggerated, gives the poem at least three levels of interpretation. His view of the past is derived from such a scholarly

familiarity that he moves with great ease and freedom in the remote period. He has sympathy for the ascetic rigors of the Celtic
Church in its earlier forms and finds in them reflections of puri-
tanical Catholicism in his own time. And when the earlier church
grew rich he finds in its various manifestations of complacent
power convenient analogies for the Irish Church of his own time
and its treatment of the individual. Insofar as its excesses are
unattractive, he can be satirical about them and use them as
absurdly magnifying mirror-images for his own age. And when
the individual, particularly the poet, is rejected by the early
Church or State, he can present him in terms of the poet's position
in modern society and comment upon his treatment at the hands
of authority.

"Celibacy" handles the problem of sexual temptation from the
point of view of the intensely ascetic individual. Other poems,
"The Confession of Queen Gormlai" and "The Young Woman of
Beare," work from the point of view of the individual who has
not mortified the flesh and restrained natural instinct. Both poems
are about women who have loved well, despite their awareness
of clerical disapproval. The second poem is a humorous take-off
on the traditional lament of the Old Woman of Beare who grieves
for her seven ages of lost youth. "The Young Woman of Beare"
proudly and consciously personifies beauty and desirable love-
liness; she is the allegorical figure of the temptation seen by
the hermit and she scorns "praying people."

> I am the bright temptation
> In talk, in wine, in sleep.
> Although the clergy pray,
> I triumph in a dream.[5]

The lament centers on her inability to repress or withstand desire. She is burdened with the inescapable vitality of her human
nature and doomed to an almost everlasting youth, to seven ages
of passion: "I flourish where desire is/And still, still I am young"[6]
The poem alternates between her proud realization of her
power as she recalls her sexual triumphs and her use of the same
experiences as moral examples to restrain other women. Her
fear of clerical disapproval and her realization of guilt, however,
is not tragic; the poem presents her as a symbol of the bright
temptation to which men are forever attracted. Thus, "Celibacy" and "The Young Woman of Beare" dramatize the two
sides of the eternal conflict: the hermit has chosen the path of
isolation, mortification, fasting, prayer, and the curbing of natural

pleasure, and the young woman has made passion supreme, a natural and desirable part of self-expression and fulfillment. They represent the extreme ends of a conflict to which almost all of Clarke's work is directed.

Pilgrimage is interesting not only in its presentation of the medieval scene and its dramatic confrontation of church teaching and natural law, but also because it shows Clarke's personal handling of metrical patterns based on Gaelic assonance and consonance. It was A.E. who first reminded him of William Larminie's theory that Gaelic assonance could be used in English to modulate rhyme. Clarke explains that in its simplest form Gaelic prosody allows the tonic word at the end of a line to be supported by an assonance in the middle of the next line. In some forms only one part of a double-syllable word is used in assonance, providing partial rhyme and muting. Poetry of this kind, he feels, "can have rhyme or assonance, on or off accent, stopped rhyme, (e.g. ring, kingdom; breath, method), harmonic rhyme (e.g. hero, window), cross-rhyme."[7] His poem "The Scholar" illustrates some of these experiments.

> Summer delights the scholar
> With knowledge and reason.
> Who is happy in hedgerow
> Or meadow as he is?
>
> Paying no dues to the parish,
> He argues in logic
> And has no care of cattle
> But a satchel and stick.
>
> The showery airs grow softer,
> He profits from his ploughland
> For the share of the schoolmen
> Is a pen in hand . . .[8]

He uses assonance sparingly and avoids the monotony so often found in Gaelic poetry of the Seventeenth and Eighteenth Centuries and the staccato effect Gaelic devices can produce when used in English. It provides him with an ancient, distinctly Irish style whose internal disciplines seem particularly suited to express his emotional and mental complexity.

The next book of poems, *Night and Morning* (1938), is the most significant of the collection. Here Clarke faces up to his own personal problems and to the problems encountered by men of his temperament in the restrictive society of post-revolutionary Ireland. Here he joins company with men like Liam O'Flaherty, Frank O'Connor, and Sean O'Faolain, whose work exemplifies a similar romantic feeling for the traditional life of the western seaboard and a similar analytical dislike for the newer forms of native middle-class consciousness emerging in the towns and cities.

The title poem, "Night and Morning," brings out a personal statement of great anguish, as he comes from behind the mask of the hermit or the natural woman and speaks directly of his "tormented soul."[9] The poem is a celebration of pride and intellect, in which Christ's suffering is used as an intellectual image. But its assertion of the dignity of the mind is made by a man in whom the familiar conflict of faith and reason is complicated: he has been reared in the Catholic faith and remains atavistically drawn to it even while the problems of adult life together with the questioning of his mind make simple acceptance no longer possible. There is a deliberate opposition in the poem between a religion that depends on mystery, on ritual, and on faith and a religion which was able to include an intellectual faith won out of argument and dispute.

> Unlocked by the secular hand,
> The very elements remain
> Appearances upon the altar.
> Adoring priest has turned his back
> Of gold upon the congregation.
> All saints have had their day at last.
> But thought still lives in pain.

It is a complicated and painful poem working consciously against the Counter-reformation, preferring a time when logic could be offered as devotion. It formulates Clarke's stand with integrity: he refuses to accept the imposition of an authority that denies reason and insists on simple faith. For him the ritualistic re-enactment of the Mass does not transcend the appearances; bread and wine do not become the body and blood of Christ, and the priest, turning his back upon the people, makes no allowances for those in the agony of doubt. By contrast, Clarke offers the "holy rage of argument" that once brought men to God.

> O when all Europe was astir
> With echo of learned controversy,
> The voice of logic led the choir.
> Such quality was in all being,
> The forks of heaven and this earth
> Had met, town-walled, in mortal view
> And in the pride that we ignore,
> The holy rage of argument,
> God was made man once more.

In these poems Clarke takes his place not as a Protestant but as a heretic within the Catholic Church. It is not an easy position. The risks in terms of eternal life are great. "God only knows," he says, "what we must suffer to be lost."[10] For such a man there is no simple solution, no possibility of total rejection. He does not rest easily on private judgment and remains in the ambivalent position of being drawn to the Church by instinct, training, and emotional need. At the same time he finds himself excluded from the comforts of the Church by his strong intellect and the demands of logic and argument. "Tenebrae" expresses his position by dramatizing the condition of a man still very much attracted to what he partially rejects. The setting is Holy Week, particularly Spy Wednesday, Holy Thursday, and Good Friday when the Church commemorates the passion and death of Christ and his sacrifice for the salvation of mankind. All crucifixes and religious statues are draped as a sign of mourning; during the evening devotions of Tenebrae a triangular candelabrum is lighted and the candles extinguished singly as the hours of Christ's suffering are remembered.

The first stanza presents the mournful ceremonies and the draped images but instead of being wrapped in the general mood Clarke poses a harrowing question:

> . . . . yet who dare pray
> If all in reason should be lost,
> The agony of man betrayed
> At every station of the cross?[11]

For the man whose reason makes it difficult to accept the proofs of God's existence, the penalty is uncertainty, isolation, and a lonely pride. Christ in his agony prayed more fervently, but intellectual doubt cannot easily be overcome by prayer. In stanza 2 Clarke poignantly remembers his childhood innocence, the period before the age of reason, but that memory does not comfort now. He combines the present occasion with the initial Lenten day, Ash Wednesday, when the priest marked the sign of the cross with ashes on the people's foreheads to remind them of mortality. Thus all occasions inform against him as assaults upon his isolation and his painful knowledge of being outside the "fold."

The third stanza shifts dramatically to the figure of Martin Luther nailing his theses to the door or Wittenberg in a symbol of intellectual integrity and individual liberty. But the identification of poet and protester is not complete.

I hammer on that common door,
Too frantic in my superstition,
Transfix with nails that I have broken,
The angry notice of the mind.
Close as the thought that suffers him,
The habit every man in time
Must wear beneath his ironed shirt.

Faced with isolation and responding to the pressure of the response of those within the fold, Clarke succumbs to "superstition,"
to the attraction of the remembered and simple, childlike faith.
At the same time, he cannot deny his reason and the conflict
goes on. "An open mind," as he states in the fourth stanza,
"disturbs the soul." He is faced with darkness, the dark night
of the soul, the impartial attraction of a religion that denies
reason, the ever-approaching darkness of death, the mystery of
the afterlife, and the possibility of being cast into exterior darkness forever. As the candles go out, the intensity of this realization grows, and the poem ends with the image of the sun always
lighting only half the world.

In other poems, Clarke continues to examine his relationship
with the Church. "Repentance" looks back wistfully to the time
when he found release and escape from his problem in the west
of Ireland—"I felt/Repentance gushing from the rock"[12]—and
states that when intellectual doubt brings spiritual despair one has
only prayer left. "Martha Blake" is a gentle portrait of a pious
woman whose life and devotion are uncomplicated. It opposes
to her the figure of Lucifer, cast from Heaven to make room for
people like her. She is happily unaffected by such an idea—"the
flame in heart is never grieved/That pride and intellect were cast
below."[13] Many poems, here and later, contrast the greater
natural freedom that once existed in Ireland. "The Lucky Coin"
looks back to pre-revolutionary days, when there was greater
individual independence. And Douglas Hyde's Love Songs of
Connaught had given plenty of evidence of greater freedom—
"Lovers forgot on the mountainside/The stern law of the
clergy."[14] "The Straying Student" asserts a belief in natural
expression. It is an account of a poor eighteenth-century
scholar who went abroad to study for the priesthood in the
Irish seminary at Salamanca but returned a spoiled priest. He
has lost his faith but has discovered the Renaissance, represented
here as a visionary woman drawing him away from the Church
to the glories of art. His only fear is that she may leave him.

> And leave me in this land, where every mother's son
> Must carry his own coffin and believe
> In dread, all that the clergy teach the young.[15]

Clarke has had the courage of his convictions and maintains his position honestly. At the same time he is clear-eyed about what he is doing. "No Recompense" measures the price he pays for his devotion to art and the working out of his personal problems—"I have endured/The enmity of my own mind that feared/no argument"[16]—and the possibility of mortal acclaim does not make up for the difficulty of that position.

Many of these poems are concerned with the conflict between the desire for freedom of action and self-expression and the regulations of the Church. The most personal, dominated by religious images and the contrasting images of natural freedoms, are the result of a genuine spiritual need. Clarke is inescapably attracted to the idea of sin, guilt, and damnation; he cannot ignore conscience and feels the need for repentance. The stern morality and the simple faith of the Irish Church fail to satisfy his needs. But his work is not limited to a self-centered interest. It is human and passionate in its concern for the dignity of man. His identification with the spoiled priest who embraced the Renaissance is not casual or accidental. It lies at the heart of his work. He is concerned with the outcast, the misfit, the mistreated, and with the individual who does not conform or blend with his environment. As well as his own religious and sexual problems there is his awareness that the drama of the individual soul is very often the drama of the racial conscience. He knows that the difficulties he experiences represent more than personal condition. Others are likely to feel the same influences and be disturbed by the same tendencies. Since the courageous and painful poetry of *Night and Morning,* his sense of public responsibility has become more pronounced. The ancient Irish bards were concerned with public utterance, with eulogy, satire, and elegy, and in the final three books of *Later Poems—Ancient Lights* (1955), *Too Great A Vine* (1957), and *The Horse-Eaters* (1960)—Clarke has written much satirical comment on public issues and events. He has moved away from the middle ages as a setting and concentrates on his own time.

The method in these poems is generally direct statement; the mood is sometimes bitter, sometimes crabby, sometimes wry; and sometimes he succeeds in making an occasional poem rise above its subject. His acceptance of local issues and events of slight importance has many explanations. One of the most interesting is found in his reference to a somewhat eccentric ancestor:

> A great-grandfather of mine, who was a skinner, lived in the Liberties of Dublin and had a tannery in Watling Street, near Usher's Quay. In his later years he seems to have become eccentric for he wore wigs of a different colour during the week. He amused himself by writing occasional verses of a satiric kind about his fellow-traders and got the ballad-singers from Thomas Street to recite them outside their shop-doors.[17]

While Clarke has not begun to wear wigs of different color, even in a symbolic sense, he has amused himself for about ten years in publishing satiric comments on local affairs. His war of words with Church and State has embraced such subjects as contraception, the follies of politicians and clergymen, censorship, airplane pilgrimages to Lourdes, the Abbey Theater, and cruelty to horses. The worse failing of these poems is that they are sometimes so concentrated in method and so full of oblique and hidden allusions to contemporary and historical occurrences that even the Irish reader has difficulty in unraveling all the meanings. It is private poetry but the game can be played by more than one. "Celebrations" is perhaps an extreme example, but it does reveal the kind of difficulty one encounters.

> Who dare complain or be ashamed
> Of liberties our arms have taken?
> For every spike upon that gateway,
> We have uncrowned the past:
> And open hearts are celebrating
> Prosperity of church and state
> In the shade of Dublin Castle.
>
> So many flagpoles can be seen now
> Freeing the crowd, while crisscross keys,
> On yellow-and-white above the green,
> Treble the wards of nation.
> God only knows what treasury
> Uncrams to keep each city borough
> And thoroughfare in grace.
>
> Let ageing politicians pray
> Again, hoardings recount our faith,
> The blindfold woman in a rage
> Condemns her own for treason:
> No steeple topped the scale that Monday
> Rebel souls had lost their savings
> And looters braved the street.[18]

The elaborate internal structure here, with its compressed and suggestive use of word, is very much in the manner of *Finnegans Wake*. There are all kinds of things one needs to know before the poem begins to make much sense, and the range of meanings is so large that it is virtually impossible to do more than suggest some of the more obvious. The notes help a little. One commentator stated that the occasion is the Dublin Eucharistic Congress of 1932 and noted that the Papal colors are yellow and white, with cross keys, while the Irish flag is green, white, and yellow. In his own notes Clarke seems to accept that and adds a few aids of his own; he points out that the Rebellion started on Easter Monday 1916, that there is a statute of Justice over the gateway of Dublin Castle, that seventy Republicans were executed during the Civil War by the Provisional Government, that when the Republican Government was in power (1936-46), of the small group of political intransigents, four were shot without trial, four were shot by firing squad, one was hanged by Pierpoint, and three died on hunger strike.[19] But these notes are not fully adequate. The celebrations are more likely those that took place on the twenty-fifth anniversary of the Rising. The presence of Papal flags is not unusual; they are frequently displayed. In addition to these general references there are more particular ones.

Thus, in the first line two patriotic songs are echoed, one—"Who Fears to Speak of Ninety-Eight"—dealing with the Insurrection of 1798, and one—"Easter Week (the Song of 1916)", which begins "Who fears to speak of Easter Week,"—dealing with the Easter Rising. The word "arms" in line 2 refers to the Rising itself and also to the executions mentioned by Clarke. There is also an anticipation of the protective powers of Church and State and possibly an implication of sexual liberties. Line 3 is an allusion to the old custom of putting rebel heads on spikes over the gateway to Dublin Castle, former headquarters of British Rule in Ireland, to discourage further rebellion. Line 4 refers to the winning of independence, the removal of the Crown or British rule, the transformation in the coinage, the removal of the rebel heads, and the disappearance of the heroic spirit they represented. The last three lines, serving as a conclusion to the gathering implications of these various meanings, point to the smugness of modern Ireland, its self-contented prosperity, and the rapport between civil and religious authority. "Open hearts" is a reflection on the mood of the occasion, a reference to the banners of the Sacred Heart on display, and a comment on the modern idea of celebrating prosperity and forgetting the "liberties." Formerly men fought and died for national independence; now they take liberties that abuse that hard-won independence. "Shade" points to the fact that Dublin Castle is no longer a stronghold of alien misrule and domination, but with its secondary meaning of "ghost," suggests that native control has brought about a new kind of oppression. Men's heads are no longer placed on show, still there are executions.

In stanza 2, the first four lines comment on the overabundance of symbols of power and uses the word "freeing" ironically and in contrast with the kind of freedom achieved by the patriots of 1916. The union of triple-colored flags, with the ecclesiastical colors in the ascendancy, explains one meaning of "treble." Another meaning also looks forward to "scale" in the last stanza, and comments on the harmony of the two powers with the humorous implication that the blend is shrill. But "wards" is perhaps most typical of Clarke's favorite device of the multiple meaning. Its primary meaning in this context is that of a district or division in a city, connecting here with "borough" and "thoroughfare," but the word is also used to signify divisions in a hospital or mental institution. "Wards" is also associated with guardianship and connects here with Church and State. But it is worth remembering that in this context the word has the meaning of a child or incompetent person. In both cases, therefore, the description of the authority of the two powers over the various sections of the nation is associated with the idea of an authoritarianism that denies the people adult and independent action. A final and supporting subtlety lies in the conjunction of "crisscross keys" and "wards," since in the craft of lock-making a "ward" is the projecting ridge in a keyhole, or lock face that permits only the right key to enter. "God only knows," Clarke observes colloquially, troubled by the sense of compacted power and secrecy on the part of the two powers, how much money it takes to keep them going. Again the upkeep of such a state is a burden on the people, a further limitation on their freedom. And "green," one remembers, can also refer to College Green, site of the Irish House of Parliament (1792-1800), before the infamous Act of Union—another uncrowning of the past, following upon the 1798 Insurrection and the military terrorism it evoked—and home now of the Bank of Ireland, a national "treasury."

Stanza 3 summarizes and comments on the contrast between 1916 and what followed upon independence. There has been a change in mood and spirit; the leaders have grown old; religious and political "faith" is now reckoned in terms of cash in a self-centered and calculated way. The Paudeens have come into their own and, like Yeats, Clarke commends the wasteful virtues of those who died without counting the cost. "The blindfold woman," Justice, standing above the gateway of Dublin Castle, where rebel heads were often displayed, now condemns the new age for its treasonable reversal of values and its self-satisfied celebrations. The Easter Rising was strictly nationalistic and was not controlled by the Church. Rebels risked life and possessions and the people had the courage to loot, as in a captured city. Now the word "loot" is given a sly secondary meaning when associated with corrupt officials.

"Celebration," therefore, formulates a striking and effective satirical contrast between the ideals and values of the past and those of the present, although it must be admitted that it loses in satirical intensity by the intricate method of its presentation.

There are times, however, when Clarke's anger is more direct, as in the group "Three Poems about Children," dealing with the burning of an orphanage in County Cavan, when sixty children died. Here his indignation, like Voltaire's, is roused by the horror of the event and the cold casuistry of a local bishop—"Has not a Bishop declared/That flame-wrapped babes are spared/Our life-time of temptation?"[20]   In contrast to the remote manipulation of allusion and connotation found in "Celebrations" and other poems, the method here is direct and forceful. First of all he reacts to the unenlightened treatment of illegitimate children at a time of national plenty. It would be better he says vehemently, to have the Church and people persecuted as in the Penal Days, when Masses were said outdoors and in secrecy. Better that than the present lack of human feeling.

> Better the book against the rock
> The misery of roofless faith,
> Than all this mockery of time
> Eternalising of mute souls.

He protests also against the theory that unbaptized children go to Limbo for eternity and are forever excluded from Paradise. His general intention is to condemn a way of life capable of callous, inhuman action. He dislikes abstract generalizations that obscure individual sufferings; he dislikes the reliance on faith to the exclusion of reason, the assumption that "smoke of faith on fire/Can hide us from enquiry." The poem ends sarcastically in a paraphrase of the episcopal casuistry, and Clarke, pretending to obey, tries to stifle his heartfelt pity for the children, and directs his mind to accept the bishop's consolatory logic. After all, he concludes in stinging irony, "Those children, charred in Cavan/Passed through Hell to Heaven."

Such poems transcend their occasions and speak openly. Another example of his ability to hit directly at signs of public insensitivity is his poem "Knacker-Rhymes," which speaks against the cruel treatment of horses being shipped out of Ireland. Protection societies, instead of condemning the trade completely, advocated the advantages of slaughtering the animals and starting a lucrative trade in horse meat. Clarke's reaction is Swiftian. Seeming to accept the materialistic logic of the societies for the prevention of cruelty—"Irishmen/Taste your own horses"—he writes,

> Don't ship, kill, can them
> First—abattoirs pay—
> Or chill the carcasses
> For hook and tray.
> Packed, sacked, quay-stacked,
> The neighless all saved
> From wavetops, ill treatment
> Abroad.[21]

The last three books, however, are not devoted exclusively to occasional pieces. Each book contains one major poem of autobiographical interest. "Ancient Lights," in the book of the same title, is a statement about his discovery of the beauty and freedom of nature after a childhood harrowed by fear, guilt and nightmare. "The Loss of Strength" in *Too Great A Vine* —the title comes from a line in the poem—is a complex poem dealing with his own relationship to the past and the present. "The Hippophagi" in *The Horse-Eaters* views the treatment of the animals in the light of a general moral condition and sees their replacement by scientific advances as part of his own history. Autobiographical reflection and investigation have been present in much of his recent work. *Twice Round the Black Church* (1962) relates some of the major influences in his growth and development. *Forget-Me-Not* (1962) is a lyrical evocation of childhood memories associated in particular with horse-carriage days in Dublin. The disappearance of the horse in recent times and his mistreatment at the hands of people motivates a gentle and sad reminder of the horse's prominent role through the centuries and his symbolical position in classical and Celtic mythology. The poem ends by equating Ireland's abuse of the horse with the destructive tendencies of armed countries. His disappearance represents a general hardening of men's hearts: "all the gentling, custom of mind/And instinct, close affection, done with."[22]

The association of insensitivity in the public conscience with the replacement of the horse by mechanical forces is part of Clarke's image for post-revolutionary Ireland. The poet's liking for the horses of Apollo, Pegasus, and the Sign of the Sagittary on the royal arch of Cormac's chapel in Cashel brings about an identification and an attitude of striking validity. "The Loss of Strength" is probably the most significant of these autobiographical poems, since it contains much personal history and effectively blends private incidents with public events. It is a sad, reflective, occasionally humorous and quietly courageous poem in which the inroads of industrial and scientific expansion ruthlessly destroy the surviving symbols of the medieval past and the freedom of the poet. A little stream in a Dublin suburb, surviving the encroachment of progress, is a symbol of the dwindling power of the past. Sadly, he associates, with the external manifestations of cultural atrophy, the restrictions age and a weakening body have placed upon his movements. He recalls his youthful pilgrimages, "when hope was active," to various places in the countryside associated with medieval Ireland.

> The young must have a solitude
> To feel the strength in mind, restore
> Small world of liking. Saints have spewed
> Too much. I wanted test of stories
> Our poets have talked about . . .[23]

The contemporary power of the Irish Church, its centralizing effect, parallels the historical intrusion of the Continental Church and the coming of the Normans. The poem has many allusions to the past, to the round towers, the hermit beds, the great stone crosses, the ruined churches. Ironically, the miracles of the Celtic saints anticipated some of the scientific marvels of the twentieth century—"No pacts/With Nature diverted river, raises up/Lake." Now, however, places sacred with memories of the Ossianic heroes are disturbed by hydroelectrical projects. The restraints imposed by science are matched by the restrictions imposed by religion. Engineering "Directs, monk-like, our natural flow," and celibacy is in vogue again. A union of Church and

State, faith and science, prevails, and the poet still prefers the past, where he "saw God's light through ruins."

The quiet humor and gentle irony of the recent autobiographical poems attest Clarke's courage through the years. Burdened with great difficulties in his personal life and harassed by frustrations in the life of the country, he has continued to produce poetry, prose, and drama of distinction. His work as a whole is a skillful, varied, and complex response to his own time, and while the later poetry is only a part of that achievement, it can serve as evidence of his imaginative range and technical ability.

Notes

1 Frank O'Connor, "The Future of Irish Literature," *Horizon,* V, (January 1942), p. 58.

2 Austin Clarke, *Twice Round the Black Church* (London: Routledge and Kegan Paul, 1962), p. 14.

3 *Ibid.,* p. 169.

4 Austin Clarke, *Later Poems* (Dublin: Dolmen Press, 1961), p. 3.

5 *Ibid.,* p. 14.

6 *Ibid.,* p. 18.

7 Austin Clarke, *Poetry in Modern Ireland* (Dublin: Sign of the Three Candles, 1961), p. 42.

8 *Later Poems,* p. 12.   This poem, found in *The Son of Learning* (1927), is a free paraphrase of an anonymous Gaelic poem, "An Mac Leighinn." But its assonantal pattern is very close to the classical meter of the original.

9 *Later Poems,* p. 29.

10 *Ibid.,* p. 30.

11 *Ibid.,* p. 31.

12 *Ibid.,* p. 34.

13 *Ibid.,* p. 33.

14 *Ibid.,* p. 36.

15 *Ibid.,* p. 37.

16 *Ibid.,* p. 38.

17 *Ibid.,* p. 92.   A slightly different account is given in *Twice Round the Black Church,* p. 13.

18 *Later Poems,* p. 43.

19 *Ibid.,* p. 91.

20 *Ibid.,* p. 46.

21 *Ibid.,* p. 74.

22 Austin Clarke, *Forget-Me-Not* (Dublin: Dolmen Press, 1962), p. 11.

23 *Later Poems,* p. 62-63.

The Private Pilgrimage of Austin Clarke

William John Roscelli

The revival of interest in the poetry of Austin Clarke, occasioned largely by the 1961 publication of his *Later Poems,* has brought into rather sharp focus one of the most difficult problems with which the literary critic has to wrestle, namely, the relative obscurity of much contemporary poetry. Obscurity does not necessarily imply a failure on the part of the poet to give adequate expression to his theme; what it connotes is more the failure of sensitive, well-disposed readers to make any meaningful penetration into the core of what is presumably an adequate piece of work. That much of Clarke's recent poetry is obscure has been conceded on virtually all sides. In *Ancient Lights* (1955), *Too Great a Vine* (1957), and *The Horse-Eaters* (1960) he makes few, if any, concessions to his readers. To be sure, not all of the poems in these volumes are difficult. For example, the intent and meaning of the sonnets "Intercessors" and "Irish-American Dignitary" are only too painfully transparent. But generally speaking it is only the weaker poems—one would hesitate to describe them as pedestrian—that yield their meaning readily. The more significant efforts—particularly "Celebrations," "Ancient Lights," "The Loss of Strength," and "The Hippophagi"—are so complex in meaning, so concentrated in form, so crammed with personal and parochial allusions, as to tax the strength of even the most resolute reader. Admittedly, once the reader has done the spadework he will be rewarded by a rich experience.

Nevertheless, in evaluating Clarke's later poetry, the critic must ask how successful is a body of work which demands that a reader be familiar with the contents of *Twice Round the Black Church* (published, incidentially, two years after *The Horse-Eaters*), the author's own notes on his poetry, as well as the coming and goings of the Irish politicians and clergy during the 'fifties before he can hope to come to terms with it. The earlier Clarke made no such demands upon his audience. One could, for example, read "The Confession of Queen Gormlai" (*Pilgrimage,* 1929) with understanding, pleasure, and profit even though he had no knowledge of Ireland, its history, or its legends.

Even as late as 1938, in such moving poems as "Night and Morning," "Tenebrae," and "The Straying Student," Clarke writes with sufficient clarity and directness, chooses his images and symbols with such care that a reader coming to his work for the first time is able quickly to establish rapport. And it is Clarke's triumph that his apparently simple lines communicate an experience which is at once profound and complex.

The fact is that in the *Collected Poems* (1935) and *Night and Morning* (1938) the poet exhibited characteristics which were in themselves almost certain proof against obscurity. His delicate and graceful similes,

> rainfall
> Was quite as the turning of books
> In the holy schools at dawn[1]

and his witty, although not quite metaphysical comparisons,

> O she turned
> So gracefully aside, I thought her clothes
> Were flame and shadow while she slowly walked,
> Or that each breast was proud because it rode
> The cold air as the wave stayed by the swan[2]

did something more than illumine a particular setting or event. They challenged our imaginations to test their appropriateness against the truth of our own experience. And because we could remember the sound of light morning rain, because we had at one time known a girl whose clothes were "flame and shadow," whose breasts had ridden "the cold air as the wave stayed by the swan," we could participate in those experiences which the poet would share with us.

In like manner, the graphic economy with which he described both scene and action in short, pulsating lines which nonetheless retained the natural quality of familiar speech gave to his poetry an air of immediate reality. The following passage is from "The Young Woman of Beare":

> Heavily on his elbow,
> He turns from a caress
> To see—as my arms open—
> The red spurs of my breast.
> I draw fair pleats around me
> And stay his eye at pleasure,
> Show but a white knee-cap
> Or an immodest smile—
> Until his sudden hand
> Has dared the silks that bind me.

See! See, as from a lathe
My polished body turning!
He bares me at the waist
And now blue clothes uncurl
Upon white haunch. I let
The last bright stitch fall down
For him as I lean back,
Straining with longer arms
Above my head to snap
The silver knots of sleep.[3]

We are not merely witnesses to this scene of passion. We
share the captain's and the woman's lust. Clarke has appealed
directly to our primeval urges, to the deliciousness of sin, and
we respond with alacrity. We follow the poet with sympathy
and understanding because we too have known "the bright temptation."

Again, the way he crystallizes the universal significance of
a commonplace situation, often by a single work or phrase,
while refraining from any moral comment, gives his poetry a
special meaning and value.

Together in the dark—
Sin-fast—we can enjoy
What is allowed in marriage.[4]

The rich implications of "sin-fast," the unexpressed yet unescap-
able contrast between "we can enjoy" and "what is allowed," the
ominous qualification suggested by "in the dark"—how precisely
are the assets and debits of unhallowed love totaled up in these
three lines. This is what Clarke could once do very well: establish a precarious balance between "the bright temptation" and
"what is allowed" by Church and Society, giving to each its due
while at the same time pointing up the terrible price one had to
pay, no matter which course is followed.

Finally, there was the compassionate irony with which Clarke
unfolded the human tragedy. "The Marriage Night," tells the
story of a beautiful, rich Roman Catholic girl, married with the
pomp and splendor of a Nuptual Mass, who, after the battle of
Kinsale, sleeps with the victorious Protestants. Clarke may mock
her Church and her own hollow faith, but there are only tender-
ness and pity in his concluding lines:

O she has curbed her bright head
Upon the chancel rail
With shame, and by her side
Those heretics have lain.[5]

Perhaps more than anything else, this sympathetic understanding of the human condition—the ceaseless quest for Eden which inevitably leads us to the cloister or the bed, which makes ideals into abstractions and turns our lust to ashes, which rips away the last veil of our illusion and leaves us naked in our weakness— that made Clarke, if not a poet of the foremost rank, nevertheless a vital one for those of us who could still believe in sin.

But in the seventeen years that elapsed between *Night and Morning* and *Ancient Lights* (1955) a profound change took place in the poetic vision of Austin Clarke. Evidence of this change is found in the techniques the poet employs. The graceful simile is replaced by the very personal description,

> Still, still I remember aweful downpour
> Cabbing Mountjoy Street, spun loneliness
> Veiling almost the Protestant church,
> Two backyards from my very home.
> I dared to shelter at locked door.
> There, walled by heresy, my fears
> Were solved. I had absolved myself:
> Feast-day effulgence, as though I gained
> For life a plenary indulgence.
>
> The sun came out, new smoke flew up,
> The gutters of the Black Church rang
> With services. Waste water mocked
> The ballcock: down-pipe sparrowing,
> And all around the spires of Dublin
> Such swallowing in the air, such cowling
> To keep high offices pure: I heard
> From shore to shore, the iron gratings
> Take half our heavens with a roar.[6]

and later by the detailed photograph, annotated by the somewhat cynical historian whose eye is on the past,

> Farm-brooks that come down to Rathfarnham
> By grange-wall, tree-stop, from the hills,
> Might never have heard the rustle in barn dance,
> The sluicing, bolting, of their flour-mills,
> Nor have been of use in the steady reel
> On step-boards of the iron wheel-rim,
> For Dublin crowds them in: they wheeze now
> Beneath new pavements, name old laneways,
> Discharge, excrete, their centuries,
> Man-trapped in concrete, deeper drainage.[7]

The not-quite-metaphysical wit gives way to the well-made pun:

> Now they have taken off their stockings
> And bared the big toe like a monk,
> Warned by the figuring of thin frock

> And belt, modesty must look up—
> Only to meet so pure a glance
> The ancient sermon will not fit,
> Since right and wrong, though self-important
> Forget the long and short of it.[8]

The natural speech patterns which marked the earlier lyrics are in the later poems replaced by clipped, compressed, almost artificial expression in which the amenities of article and conjunction are frequently dispensed with.

> The young must have a solitude
> To feel the strength in mind, restore
> Small world of liking. Saints have spewed
> Too much. I wanted test of stories
> Our poets had talked about, pinmeal
> To potboil long ago. Cloud-feelers
> Featherers, touched our restlessness.
> Lost prosody restrained us. Summit
> showed valleys, reafforesting,
> The Fianna, leaf-veined, among them.[9]

The Young Woman of Beare never spoke like that.

Concomitant with these changes in technique is a shift in attitude. In his earlier poems, Clarke appeared deliberately to refrain from making moral judgments; in the later poems, by comparison, he seems almost dogmatic.

> Better to disobey
> And keep her alive than pray
> To scissors and rubber glove
> So quickly again. Not love
> But faith blesses our dust
> In passing. Take cover: trust
> No fit of Caesar. Knife
> Killed him, brought to life.[10]

More important, the spirit of compassion which informed so much of Clarke's earlier work is in the later poems replaced by the austere objectivity of a disinterested observer or by the wry amusement of one in whom the fires of passion have been banked.

> Pity poor lovers who may not do what they please
> With their kisses under a hedge, before a raindrop
> Unhouses it; and astir from wretched centuries,
> Bramble and brier remind them of the saints. . . .
> Lying in the grass as if it were a sin
> To move, they hold each other's breath, tremble,
> Ready to share that ancient dread—kisses begin
> Again—of Ireland keeping company with them.[11]

To be sure, there are occasional flashes of the old Clarke, especially in "Three Poems about Children," the second of which poignantly comments on the official Catholic attitude concerning infants who die without benefit of Baptism:

> Though faith allow
> Obscurity of being
> And clay rejoice: flowers
> That wither in the heat
> Of benediction, one
> By one, are thrown away.[12]

But such moments are relatively rare in the *Later Poems*.

Finally, there is a marked change in the tone of Clarke's satire. The earlier poems had mocked gently, and almost invariably with humor, those institutions and practices which had won his disapproval. In the *Later Poems*, particularly in *Too Great a Vine* and *The Horse-Eaters*, he sounds a much harsher note. While his satire stings rather than lacerates, the pain it evokes is sharp enough to cause more than a passing wince. The poet himself is acutely aware of this shift. In his notes to *Too Great A Vine* he remarks, "In their notices of *Ancient Lights: Poems and Satires, First Series,* a few critics suggested that some of the pieces were too mild to be called satires. I hope that I have made amends."[13] But the increase in acerbity does not make his satire more effective. The art by which Clarke, like Donne before him, had once mirrored the most significant of human actions in the most commonplace of events is almost totally absent now. The poet seems content to ridicule the ephemeral actions of clergymen, politicians, and meat-packers without clearly relating them to deep-seated human vices and follies. The result is that the reader who does not have Clarke's notes frequently fails to understand what the fuss is all about. And even when he has uncovered the objects of attack in such poems as "Mother and Child," "Local Complainer," and "Knacker Rhymes," the reader must consider whether the experience has been worth the trouble.[14]

What these changes in technique, tone, and perspective suggest is not a decline in poetic power but a retreat from public poetry. The specific events in Clarke's personal life which may have occasioned the retreat belongs properly to the province of biography, although I suspect Clarke has told us a great deal about it in "The Loss of Strength." However, it is the critic's function to describe as precisely as possible the change revealed by his poetry itself, and in the *Later Poems* what is most apparent is the poet's withdrawal from the flesh. The best of Clarke's earlier work dealt with the conflict between flesh and spirit, between man's primeval urges and the demands imposed by a conscience that has been conditioned by religion and morality. But in these poems of conflict it was Clarke's treatment of the flesh which gave his lyrics vitality and power. For confirmation of this judgment, we need only look at a poem like "The Young Woman of Beare." The form of the poem, considered in the abstract, demands that a balance be struck between the pleasure she derives from the memory of past physical delights and the suffering she endures, prompted by the awareness that she has no spiritual resources from which she can draw consolation once her body has become decrepit. But actually the poem works another way. Its strength lies in those stanzas of passion which describe the "bright temptation"; it is their intensity which gives the quasi-didactic passages meaning. What we feel when we read the woman's warnings to young girls is an acute sense of loss. We are, in fact, confronted with a reversal of the Epicurean proposition that pleasure is the absence of pain; for the Young Woman of Beare pain is the absence of pleasure. She may "fear, lost and late,/The prelates of the Church," but the moral she preaches is that a woman who does not give herself over to pleasure in her youth will not keenly feel its absence in old age. But then she will not have the Woman of Beare's memories either, and those memories are too moving for us really to wish she had been denied the experiences which gave them birth. Thus, in its total effect, the poem does not achieve the balance which in theory we had expected. We feel regret but not remorse. What we would give the Woman of Beare, had we the power, is not spiritual consolation but perpetual youth. And perpetual youth is precisely what Clarke gives her. She remains forever the "bright temptation" to lure us into sin, and we willingly yield ourselves to her with some fear perhaps but not remorse—our flesh is too much with us.

Remorse of a sort is suggested in the less cleanly etched "Confession of Queen Gormlai," who describes herself as "impure with love." Dying in a hovel, forsaken by all, clad only in rags, the once beautiful woman enumerates the sins which she feels have brought her to this pitiable condition. But as we read her narrative we experience no sense of evil. She has tasted fully the pleasures which life has to offer and she lingers fondly over the details of her marriages with Cormac and Niall; she recalls with sadness the now lost splendor of castle life. She rebukes herself for her pride, her weakness, and her lust, thereby justifying the terrible retribution which God has visited upon her; nevertheless, we feel that she is more a victim than a sinner, a woman wronged by gods and men. And she herself unconsiously implies that the sense of guilt which torments her in her final hours has been induced by others: her father, the clergy, the philosophers. She gave herself to life willingly, without guile; and because she did yield to her natural impulses, she has been destroyed as those whom she has loved were destroyed before her. This is the tragic way of the world, Clarke suggests; the savage God of Genesis remains with us.

But for all the pity it may evoke, "The Confession of Queen Gormlai" does not provide a fair representation of the conflict between flesh and spirit. Gormlai is too much the innocent responsive woman to experience, much less understand, the struggle between conscience and desire. Her shame, her remorse are consequent upon the suffering she endures. They exist only in retrospect. It remains for the speaker in "Celibacy" to delineate the conditions of the conflict between primeval and sophisticated man in its starkest terms. The speaker is ostensibly an ascetic, a monk perhaps, but we immediately recognize him as the prototype of civilized man, who has accepted without equivocation the dogmas of the social order of which he is a member. Nevertheless, there still surge within him those primitive instincts which cannot be subdued or modified by precept and convention. Manfully the speaker wrestles with his own desires, appealing to his God for aid, but the help that comes is illusory. He must ultimately depend upon his own strength to combat his adversary. The result is stalemate. Flesh and spirit exhaust each other. Neither triumphs, so that the reader is left to determine for himself whether the tremendous energy consumed by this interminable battle has been futilely expended.

This probing into the nature of the struggle between flesh and spirit and its consequences for us continues to mark Clarke's poetry until the later 'thirties, when in lyrics like "Night and Morning," "Tenebrae," and "The Straying Student," we notice slight alterations in the poet's approach. The flesh is still with us, but it has been to a considerable extent chastened. What occupies Clarke now, what he yearns for, is finding some means of reconciling the warring elements. Specifically, the reconciliation he seeks is between faith and flesh. He flies back to the Middle Ages for succor.

O when all Europe was astir
With echo of learned controversy,
The voice of logic led the choir.
Such quality was in all being,
The forks of heaven and this earth
Had met, town-walled, in mortal view
And in the pride that we ignore,
The holy rage of argument,
God was made man once more.[15]

But he realizes that there are certain intellectual and emotional impediments which made the rapproachment he so fervently desires all but impossible:

I hammer on that common door,
Too frantic in my superstition,
Transfix with nails that I have broken,
The angry notice of the mind.[16]

However, as we learn from "The Straying Student," the primary stress is intellectual rather than instinctual. It is the secular vision of the universe, authenticated by centuries of human achievement, which prevents him from submitting to the theological view. So the poet knows no peace. He is only too keenly aware of the limits of human achievement, the hollowness of human consolation; yet he feels too strongly the pull of the "good" life, the full life, to negate its riches and embrace the austerity of other-worldliness. He can lament the pitiable condition which leaves him no alternative to despair, yet in his heart he knows that even in the Age of Faith, when "God was made man once more," the dilemma which confronts him was not resolved.

The misery of common faith
Was ours before the age of reason.
Hurrying years cannot mistake
The smile for the decaying teeth,
The last confusion of our senses.
But O to think, when I was younger
And could not tell the difference,
God lay upon this tongue.[17]

It is only the invincible ignorance of youth which can accommodate the conflicting claims of faith and reason, flesh and spirit.

In these poems from Night and Morning, Clarke relates his experience in terms far more personal than we encountered in Pilgrimage. He is forced to this expedient partly because the religious experience of each man, at least in its mystical aspects, is unique, and partly because his reaction to that experience is curiously ambivalent. He is not simply a man who has lost or changed his faith; rather he is a man who finds to his horror that he cannot reconcile *his* mature experience with *his* youthful faith. What he craves to recapture before all else is the emotional quality of his early religious experience, to enjoy once more the security his childhood faith had given him. But the course which his mature life has followed produces upon him a psychological impact that precludes any return to the religion of his youth. Now the mature experience which places the poet in the equivocal position which he describes in *Night and Morning* is peculiarly his own. He cannot reasonably expect his readers to have lived his life. Consequently, for him to generalize from his private experience would be to distort, to dogmatize, and this Clarke wisely refrains from doing. He is content that we should respond to his personal tragedy as our own experience dictates. And because we have all known loss, uncertainty, and confusion, if not despair, our response is sympathetic, even though we may not share Clarke's particular illusions or discontents.

But in *Ancient Lights* a deeper and more troublesome personal note is sounded. The title poem is frankly autobiographical and, despite occasional brilliance in sound and imagery, it sustains our interest largely because we are concerned with how Clarke thinks and feels. The poet is rigorous in his refusal to relate his experience to our own, and rightly so, for the primary function of the lyric is to explain the metamorphosis of Austin Clarke. Insofar as we can understand his evolution, we can understand the attitudes he takes in the satires which follow the apologia. What is disturbing about "Ancient Lights," however, is that it delineates in highly compressed form a mystical experience which few readers, if any, can share. The events, the place-names, the allusions, the images which are obviously so meaningful to the poet can evoke from the reader only the vaguest sort of response. At least in *Night and Morning* there were the undercurrents of passion, the appeals to humanism and to history, and the sense of loss and insecurity to guide us; but after the third stanza of "Ancient Lights" we can follow the poet only with the greatest difficulty. We do not feel the magic effects which the birds in Rutland Square and the Black Church in Mountjoy Street wrought upon him. We are not participants in this poem; we are auditors merely. We listen and assent, or at least try to assent. Our status as auditors shapes our response to Clarke's satires as well. We recognize the nature of his protests but are hard pressed to understand what it is he finds so sinister in the petty or sterile manifestations of faith and politics that draw his ridicule. Among the better lyrics, only "Celebrations," "Three Poems About Children," and "Vanishing Irish," seem to transcend the ephemeral occasions which inspired their composition to provide us with meaningful experience.

In his introductory note to *Too Great a Vine,* Clarke comments, "As I have few personal interests left, I have concentrated on local notions and concerns which are of more importance than we are, keep us employed and last long."[18] This statement goes far to explain why from *Ancient Lights* onward the poet has focused upon certain themes, but it does not tell the whole story. Although Clarke may have few personal interests left, whatever does interest him he views through the myopic lens of his tragic personal history. And the dominating factors in his vision are disillusionment and rejection. The illusions of faith and romance which vitalized his youth have been brutally destroyed by his mature experience. He finds in his mature world, however fervently the clergy may proclaim the contrary, no personal God, no sin; only the elementary forces of power and desire exist. No saints and heroes walk among us; only prelates and politicians. But without God and sin, without saints and heroes, the conflicts between flesh and spirit, faith and reason sink into nothingness. What is left to the poet is a sterile, pragmatic society whose tastes and values he must of necessity reject. In angry despair he probes deeply into his own personal history and that of his race to secure evidence of the truth of the illusions which had once given his joy and suffering meaning. The evidence, however, is not forthcoming. The best that he can find, in the streams that flow past Rathfarnham and the noble Irish horses, are symbolic representations of ages past which cherished those illusions he has lost, symbols made all the dearer to him by the fact that both horse and stream have been barbarously treated by his contemporaries. But the symbols do not have sufficient force to satisfy Clarke's quest. To the questions the poet asks there are no final answers, a fact which he ultimately concedes in his final anguished query,

> What dare we call
> Our thought, Marcus Aurelius,
> Unwanted void or really us?[19]

We cannot descend with Clarke into his private hell. We can watch him suffer, we can sympathize with him, perhaps pity him. But we cannot share his agony. We can listen with attention to the observations that he makes about Church, State, and Society, but we cannot test their validity since we only partially understand the experiences which gave them birth. We are witnesses to a performance whose meaning and import frequently elude us, although we are often dazzled by its brilliance and intensity. We do not blame Clarke. We only wish that we might have been able to participate more fully in the experiences which the poet has attempted to communicate.

The Clarke of *Ancient Lights, Too Great a Vine,* and *The Horse-Eaters,* it becomes clear, is far removed from the Clarke of *Pilgrimage* and even of *Night and Morning.* Where the younger poet invited us to test the validity of his vision against the truth of our own experience, the later Clarke has made his personal experience the standard against which contemporary society must be judged. Where the author of *Pilgrimage* sought to find in history, myth, and legend what G. K. Chesterton would call the universal allegorical application, the later Clarke all too often seems content to describe the private microcosm that has been created from his personal history. Finally, where the younger man was relatively clear and direct, the elder poet is more often than not obscure.

A critic's reaction to the changes he finds in Clarke's later verse must, I think, necessarily be mixed. Douglas Sealy may find it "exciting that a poet should find his material in the daily life of the country,"[20] but I doubt if many readers outside Ireland (and how many in Ireland?) can generate much enthusiasm for the ephemeral and parochial themes upon which Clarke lavishes so much attention in the *Later Poems.* Further, it is questionable whether the compression for which the poet consistently strives in the later poems always serves his ends. For example, Clarke tells us that "Celebrations" is concerned with three decades of Irish politics, a fact which apparently eluded Donagh Mac-Donagh, editor of the *Oxford Book of Irish Verse,* who wrote that the poem dealt with the Dublin Eucharistic Congress of 1932.[21] Must the reader's failure to apprehend the full scope of the lyric be attributed to his own obtuseness or does the responsibility lie mainly with the poet, who has made demands upon the reader which the latter cannot reasonably be expected to meet? If Maurice Harmon's analysis of the poem is correct, it would seem that Clarke has created a puzzle which only a handful of readers could hope to resolve.[22] Also, it must be asked whether such a high degree of introspection as we find in a poem like "The Hippophagi" is artistically justifiable. Douglas Sealy brushes such questions aside with the comment that "the poet has earned the right to be obscure,"[23] which is utter nonsense. Clarke can write drivel if it pleases him to do so, but none of us is under any obligation to read it. If a writer wishes to be read, he must offer his audience some hope that it will be able to comprehend the import of his words. And it is doubtful that in some of his later poems Clarke offers us such hope.

But having made these reservations, the critic will still find much of value in Clarke's later poems. As all of us have known the "bright temptation," so each of us has made his private pilgrimage into the past in the hope of resuscitating those beloved illusions of our youth. Clarke searches for a way to live with human dignity, at peace with himself in a world that has apparently lost the traditional values that had sustained it for centuries. Specifically he seeks a faith. Insofar as his search involves an almost total rejection of the society of which he is a part and which, as he acknowledges, he has done his own bit to create, we may demur at following him. But to the extent that he points up the longings of the human spirit, man's need for faith in someone or something, we must respond empathetically to his words. In spite of his obscurity, or perhaps because of it, Clarke has succeeded in drawing a portrait of contemporary man, lonely in his isolation, confused and frightened by the horrible gap he discovers between reality as he experiences it and reality as he had imagined it.

Notes

1 "Pilgrimage," *Later Poems* (Dublin: Dolmen Press, 1961), p. 3.

2 "Aisling," *ibid.*, p. 24.

3 *Ibid.*, pp. 15-16.

4 *Ibid.*

5 *Ibid.*, p. 23.

6 "Ancient Lights," *ibid.*, pp. 48-49.

7 "The Loss of Strength," *ibid.*, p. 61.

8 "Fashion," *ibid.*, p. 43.

9 "The Loss of Strength," *ibid.*, p. 63.

10 "The Choice," *ibid.*, p. 68.

11 "The Envy of Poor Lovers," *ibid.*, p. 53.

12 *Ibid.*, p. 45.

13 *Ibid.*, p. 92.

14 *Ibid.*, pp. 60-61, 74-75. This statement, especially in regard to "Knacker Rhymes," is not wholly objective. I have seen too many people dying of starvation in Shimbashi slums to become greatly exercised over man's inhumanity to horses. If an export horse trade can boost a nation's economy and help eliminate poverty, I find nothing short-sighted or stupid in it, Lemuel Gulliver and Austin Clarke notwithstanding. See *ibid.*, p. 94.

15 "Night and Morning," *ibid.*, p. 30.

16 "Tenebrae," *ibid.*, p. 31.

17 "The Jewels," *ibid.*, p. 40.

18 *Ibid.*, p. 92.

19 "The Hippophagi," *ibid.*, p. 88.

20 *Ibid.*, p. 31.

21 *Ibid.*, p. 91, and *The Oxford Book of Irish Verse* (New York: Oxford University Press, 1958), p. xxi.

22 See Harmon's essay above.

23 "Austin Clarke: A Survey of his Work," *Dubliner*, January-February 1963, p. 17.

FOLKLORE AND POPULAR
CULTURE

Folk literature has in our time assumed singular importance as a fertile field for anthropological, historical, and literary inquiry. Sometimes the results of these inquiries, if superficially developed, are misleading. The apparent artlessness of much folk literature can deceive the unwary scholar into believing that the excellencies he finds in it derive from the natural genius of the people rather than from the craftsmanship of the anonymous authors. The distinction is fundamental when the scholar tries to disentangle the primal substance, say of a myth, embodied in a folk tale or poem from the accretions and modifications which have been introduced by later authors retelling the story for the benefit of their contemporaries. Insofar as a myth sums up a culture or a phase of a culture it will yield certain information about the history and character of the race or people whose primeval experience it crystallizes; and the folk literature in which the myth is preserved must reflect the personalities of its authors and their times.

That distinguishing between the two, especially in Irish folk literature, is difficult is demonstrated by MacEdward Leach in his essay "Matthew Arnold and 'Celtic Magic.'" He shows that such sensitive readers as Arnold and Yeats confused the artistry of the storyteller with the national characteristics of the Irish people. The effect of Arnold's error was twofold: it gave false understanding of Irish myths and legends; and it did a grave injustice to the Irish storytellers, to whose art it failed to give due recognition. That Arnold, in 1866, should have made the mistakes is not surprising. But that contemporary scholars should continue to perpetuate his errors—and similar ones—is shocking. However, as Leach points out, it is difficult to intellectualize about the elusive qualities of folk literature. One of the most effective ways to handle them is to use techniques analogous to those he uses in his essay.

Another task confronting the modern student of folk literature involves distinguishing between it and popular literature. In this connection Ray Browne's study is instructive. Precisely because popular literature attempts to capitalize upon the public mood of a moment, because its simplicity and directness are synthetic, it lacks the enduring power of folk literature which has its roots in the national heritage of a people.

For popular literature to survive it must either transcend the occasion which inspired it or it must work into the hearts of the populace and become a part of the coin of their realm. But folk or popular literature, both are immensely important in the study of history and literature, as these two papers demonstrate.

William John Roscelli

Matthew Arnold and "Celtic Magic"

MacEdward Leach

In 1866, Matthew Arnold delivered four lectures on Celtic literature at Oxford University. Central to his idea was his contention that an innate quality differentiates Celtic folk literature from the literature of other peoples. This unique quality he called Celtic Magic. His idea was predicated on the theory that race determines culture. Specifically he believed that innate national strains of melancholy, sense of beauty, spirituality, and impractibility determine Celtic literary style. Though science soon discredited the ideas of both innate culture patterns and a Celtic race, the term Celtic Magic has come to be associated with Celtic literature ever since.

Everyone who has read Celtic folk story, or has listened to Gaelic, Welsh, or even Breton, folk song, recognizes readily that such story and song do have a distinct quality—a quality difficult to pin down; it is sensed, but hard to intellectualize. Arnold's word, with its connotation of the mysterious and the occult, was eagerly seized upon by both critics and literary historians to describe this quality. The term became a commonplace. With the Irish Revival the term took on new connotations as used by the poets and the interpreters of Celtic literature. Celtic magic becomes magic indeed, for now it is used to suggest that the Celtic mind and spirit and their products not only are strange and mystical, but operate in a kind of twilight between reality and the dream, and over all broods a deep melancholy. Critics and teachers still use this term without hesitation to distinguish the Celtic temperament, and Celtic literature too, from those of England and Germany. Writers using Celtic sources form their material into this mold so that it is often more than magical; it is made into the weird and fantastic or even the bizarre. Fiona Macleod is an excellent example; and even Yeats became deeper and deeper involved in the Celtic Twilight.

It is difficult to determine exactly what Arnold meant by Celtic Magic. In discussing the peculiar quality of Celtic litera-

ture he says, "Magic is the word to insist upon, a magical,
vivid and near interpretation of nature." And in another place,
"Magic is the word for it—the magic of nature, her weird power
and her fairy charm." But just what Arnold means precisely by
this magic of nature and her weird power and fairy charm is
difficult to understand, especially in the light of his later statement in which he seems to suggest that the magic is something
added by the artist. "The eye," he says, "is on the object but
charm and magic are added." Is then the magic in the object,
or is it in the way it is viewed and presented by the Celt?
Through his third and fourth essays this confusion leaves us
wandering in a veritable Celtic Twilight.

For example, he quotes the following passage from *Geraint
and Enid*: "And early in the day Geraint and Enid left the
wood, and they came to an open country, with meadows on one
hand and men mowing the meadows. And there was a river
before them, and the horses bent down and drank the water.
And they went up out of the river by a steep bank, and there
they met a slender stripling with a sachel about his neck; and he
had a small blue pitcher in his hand, and a bowl on the mouth
of the pitcher." All of this, Arnold says, is simply clear beauty
of landscape description. The next sentence, he continues, adds
the magic: "And they saw a tall tree by the side of the river,
one half was in flames from the root to the top and the other
half was in green leaf." Here obviously the magic is in the object,
and it is a supernatural kind of magic.

Contrast this with another passage Arnold quotes to illustrate
Celtic Magic. "Is it not autumn when the fern is red, the water
flag yellow? . . . Is it not winter time now, when men talk
together after they have drunken? . . . Is it not spring when
the cuckoo passes through the air, when the foam sparkles on
the sea . . ." Here the magic has clearly been added.

That Celtic literature does have a distinct quality, no one
who knows it well will deny, but one does it an injustice to use
the word *magic* to describe it. That word is too general and
carries too many connotations. More misleading still is the
suggestion that the magic is the expression of a unique racial
temperament. Let us examine some Celtic folk literature to
see if it is not possible to arrive at a more accurate description of
their common quality.

The first illustration is a famous passage in the Deirdre
story. The old king Conchobar has just left the young girl,

Deirdre, after telling her that he will return the next year to marry her. Distressed, she sits brooding in the high window of the castle looking out over the snowy forest. The servants have just killed a calf; its blood is running out over the snow. As Deirdre looks out on the scene, a raven flies down and begins drinking the blood. Deirdre turns to her nurse, standing behind her and says: "Lavarcam, I don't want to marry an old man; I want a young man, one whose cheeks are red as the blood I see flowing out on the snow, and whose hair is as black as the raven drinking the blood, and whose body is as white as the snow."

All who read this passage I think feel its charm and its individual quality. Magic? The magic of the artist, certainly. The unforgettable quality of this passage comes from a variety of sources: its concreteness; its specific detail; its pictorial vividness: the girl at the window looking out on the snowy scene, the red blood, the black raven against the whiteness and all against the somber forest in the background. It has the sharpness of detail of medieval illumination. Moreover, the triadic structure gives it a oneness, a compactness, and a suggestion of invocation. It is as if Deirdre were saying: "I invoke the forces of nature to protect me from this old man, this alliance so against nature." Deirdre's own cheeks are red as the blood and her hair is black as the raven and her body white as the snow; Conchobar is old and gray and colorless.

Perhaps these elements do combine to evoke in the reader a feeling of magic, but it is the magic of poetry, the magic wrought by the bard, the poet, rather than by the druid, the magician. It has the same quality of magic as the following:

A voice so thrilling neer was heard
In spring-time from the Cuckoo-bird
Breaking the silence of the seas
Beyond the farthest Hebrides.
. . .
Perhaps the plaintive numbers flow
For old, unhappy far-off things
And battles long ago.

The next example is from *The Boyhood Deeds of Finn*. Demne was the boy's real name, but his nickname was Finn, fair one. Toward evening Demne came to the dark pool beside which sat the old man, Finn. Finn was very old; as he sat cross-legged beside the pool his beard flowed down to his waist, thick and very white. Intently he stared into the dark pool. Around the pool were twelve hazel trees, and on the trees were vermillion red nuts, each containing the wisdom of the world. Now and then one of the nuts would ripen and fall into the pool and a red bubble would rise through the black water and a salmon would swirl up out of the depths and swallow the red nut. For seven years the old man Finn had been trying to catch the salmon that he might eat it and so gain the knowledge of the world.

As Demne came near, the old man caught the salmon. He gave it to Demne to cook for him, cautioning him not to eat any of it. When Demne brought the cooked fish, Finn asked him if he had tasted it. Demne confessed that he had pressed down a blister on the cooking fish with his thumb and had then put the thumb in his mouth and so tasted the fish.

Then Finn said, "What is your name, lad?"

The boy answered, "Demne."

"And have you no other?" asked Finn.

"They call me Finn also," said the boy.

And then did old Finn know that this was the boy about whom the prophesy was made: Finn will eat the salmon of Knowledge and so gain the wisdom of the world. And he handed Demne the fish and said, "Eat, for indeed thou art the Finn."

And so Finn ate, and from his new wisdom he made his first song—the song of May and new life:

Bees with puny strength carry a goodly burden, the harvest of blossoms;

The harp of the forest sounds music, the sail gathers;

Color has settled on every height haze on the lake of full waters.

The corncrake, a strenuous bard, discourses; the lofty virgin water-fall sings a welcome to the warm pool.

The talk of rushes is come.

The peat bog is as the raven's coat; the loud cuckoo bids welcome; the speckled fish leaps; strong is the bound of the swift warrior.

Again we have vivid picture: the dark pool, reflecting the hazel trees covered with the red nuts, the old man with the flowing white beard, watching the red nuts fall and the red bubbles rise and waiting for the speckled fish. Here again is concreteness, realism, and a high degree of specificity. And here too is the suggestion of knowledge coming from close association with the physical world. The hazel, like the rowan, was one of the magic working trees of the Druids, and so Demne, partaking of the salmon of knowledge, which had swallowed the nut of the hazel, is prepared to lead the fianna, the band of warriors dedicated to the defense of the land. The symbolism here seems like magic, to be sure—eating the salmon of knowledge endows Demne with the gift of poetry that comes through identification with the physical world. The same ichor that runs through the veins of the oak runs through the heart of man. Or as Demne said it: "The speckled fish leaps; strong is the bound of the swift warrior." It is the great chain of being, so easy to interpret mystically by those whose gods live in heaven, but completely realistic to the Celts, whose gods dwelt on the earth.

My third example comes ultimately from a Breton source; it is the last episode in the *Lai of Eliduc.* Guillardun has fled from her country with Eliduc. But he has not told her that he is married. When she discovers it, she falls into a deep swoon so that he thinks she is dead. He wraps her purple cloak with the red lining around her and carries her to the little chapel beside the castle. The door is locked; a servant climbs up and gains entrance through the transom. Eliduc carries the lady in and gently places her on the dais at the base of the altar; her purple cloak hangs down revealing the red lining and her hair streams back from her white face. For two days he laments the girl in the chapel. In all that time she does not change, nor stir, nor breathe, and he marvels greatly, for he sees her, red and white, as he had known her in life. On the third day the lord's wife discovers the affair and goes with a servant to the chapel and there she marvels over the lady whose beauty shines like a gem. As she stands there, a weasel runs across the body, and the servant strikes it with his stick and kills it. In a few minutes the mate of the dead weasel comes and discovers it. The mate goes and returns quickly with a very red flower in her mouth; this she places on the mouth of her dead mate and immediately he stands on his feet. Then the lady shouts to the servant, "Throw, man, throw, and gain the flower." This he does and the lady takes the red flower and places it on the girl's mouth. And Guillardun opens her eyes and says: "Have I slept so long?" The lady gives thanks to God that the girl lives.

Here again is the quality that Arnold would call Celtic Magic, the sharply etched picture, the mixture of the very realistic with the very romantic (the locked door, the servant entering through the transom, the pre-Raphaelite picture of the girl lying before the altar).

These three illustrations from Celtic folk literature, though differing in time and place, have common, distinctive qualities— concrete and specific detail, no differentiation between natural and supernatural, rational and irrational, pictorial composition with constant and vivid use of color, close integration of the physical world by way of symbol and figure of speech. Other qualities are a tendency toward understatement, abstraction translated into terms of action and symbol, and animism.

These are the qualities of Celtic literature that define Arnold's phrase, "Celtic Magic." If "magic" can be used to describe these qualities, then they are magic. But certainly they are not uniquely Celtic, for they are qualities possessed by folk literature in general. They are folk magic. Folktale, epic, ballad—the folk narratives of many people show the same magic.

Consider the following:

> And they followed a road through the high mountains, a narrow road ever winding upward, and they came to a towering shining cliff, gleaming in the sun as if set with thousands of jewels, and leading up the cliff were twenty-five thousand steps, and each was linked to the one above with chains of red gold. The steps seemed carved of sapphires and rubies, giving off brilliant blue and red radiance. . . . The King mounted the steps, ever higher toward the top. And there was a great green plain. On the plain were many people clad in the skins of panthers and lions. Beyond was a palace, its dome of gold shining in the sun. Two great bronze doors led to its hall and seventy windows of different shapes were on each side. The doors were set with precious stones set in beaten gold.

> . . . and the doors slowly opened and the king saw lying on a bed was an old man with a fair face and long white hair and a long white beard flowing down. His couch was hung with bright brocade, its cover was blue, embroidered in bright gold. The bed curtains were embroidered to show a garden with trees and beasts and birds of many colors. [In a wood were] olives, cypress, cedars, and many precious trees bearing spices and incense. And there was a great tree with no leaves or bark and in its top a great bird like a peacock in color. Its head was red and its breast golden and its back and tail gold and red. . . . And the guide told him that it was the Phoenix, the bird that lives a hundred years and has no mate.

Certainly this passage possesses the magic described by Arnold. It is from the *De Proeliis* version of the Alexander. From folk story hundreds of such passages could be cited. Folk literature is characteristically concerned with concrete and specific detail, supernatural treated as rational, and the rest.

But still, there *is* a difference between Celtic folk literature and that of many other peoples. The difference is not in kind, as Arnold suggests, but in quality. Celtic folk literature is fine folk literature. The stories are better told than most; they differ not in kind but in art.

The Celts, even on the folk level, were superior as poets and story tellers. This came from the early and long-continued professional training of bard and filid and from the influence of the lore, learning, and skill of the Druids in story and song. The influence of the filid and Druid schools was felt through the middle ages even in the most isolated villages. It accounts today for such great folk-story tellers as Peig Sayers. Celtic literature from a very early period—third century, perhaps—shows a constant interplay between folk and sophisticated levels of culture. For a thousand years the stream of conscious art dipped down into the stream of folk art, and both benefited. The great art of the Deirdre story, for example, is a magnificent combination of folk art—the simple concrete picture—with the beautiful structuring and psychological motivation of sophisticated art.

Secondly, the pre-Christian Celts always identified closely with the physical world. Their world was never a place of temporary abode, a place to pass through on the way to an everlasting heaven. Their successive waves of gods dwelt on this earth; they were there through the middle ages in spite of Christianity; they may still be there in the land under the hill. The sovereignty of Ireland is no poetic commonplace; it is rather a living spirit. Out of this has come the close relation with all aspects of the physical world: the crested wave, the red berry, the speckled fish, and the three swans.

The Paine-Burke Controversy in Eighteenth-century Irish Popular Songs

Ray B. Browne

The political controversy between Thomas Paine and Edmund Burke erupted violently in Ireland, as in England, Scotland, France and America, with the publication of Burke's *Reflections on the Revolution in France,* in November 1790, and of Paine's answer, *The Rights of Man,* Part I, February 1791, and Part II, February 1792. Extracts from the *Reflections* were published in at least three Irish newspapers,[1] sections of the *Rights* in at least four.[2] Numerous "answering" pamphlets, often written by Burke's personal friends, were directed against Paine and his principles of government. Refutations of Burke were printed also, though in smaller number.[3] Ireland was in ferment over the opposing political philosophies presented by these two men.

This ferment was intensified upon the publication in 1796 of Paine's *Age of Reason.* As with the earlier work, this piece was commented on in Irish newspapers, both favorably and unfavorably. Sometimes editors who at first approved, before gauging fully their own and their readers' reaction, found themselves later recanting with a blush.[4] Thus Paine's political impact suffered a significant reversal because of what was felt to be his religious radicalism. Irish political revolutionism, to be sure, had always had overtones of anti-clericalism, but it could not accept what seemed to be the atheism espoused by Paine. Therefore in Paine, in the excesses of the French Revolution (which he presumably approved), in the supposed religious infidelity believed to be inseparably linked to it, conservatives found ammunition for their propaganda barrages against Paine personally, and against all kinds of reform and liberalism.

There were, to be sure, radicals like Arthur O'Connor and W. P. McCabe, the northern United Irishman, whose fierce anti-clericalism was blown to white heat by the *Age of Reason.* Although the conclusion is unavoidable that after the publication of this work, the majority of literate Irishmen rejected Paine in politics as well as in religion, his followers among the reading classes were determined and noisy.

And they were encouraged by Irishmen of the lower classes. The comment of radical Mrs. McTier, speaking about the *Rights,* was prophetic: "I never liked kings, and Paine has said of them what I always suspected, truth seems to dart from him in . . . plain and pregnant terms . . . and I imagine his writings will have a most important effect on the public mind." In this public mind, indeed, the principles proclaimed by Paine were heady wine. Forgetting, or being indifferent to, Paine's religious heresies, many people looked upon him as speaking for and to mankind in general, charting the road to revolution, freedom and happiness for all. Burke, on the contrary, was gall in their mouths. They felt that he begged for the opposite of everything they desired: conservatism, status quo, colonial dependence—in brief, continued servitude and misery.

Thus in the minds of many the lines of battle were drawn in the titanic struggle between conservatism and liberalism, expediency and principle, the past and the future, wretchedness and happiness.

One of the best indexes of the mind of the day is the popular and folk songs, sung by the people and reflecting their genuine feelings and opinions, or at least those that were generally accepted as their own. But the studies which treat Burke and Paine and their controversy in Ireland almost always ignore popular songs. This paper is an attempt to bridge the gap.[5]

The best depository of these songs is the popular songbooks or "songsters," as they called, of the time. These books contained up to a hundred pages, from fifty to a hundred songs set to well-known popular or folk tunes. Printed on cheap paper and selling for a pittance, they were indeed man's companion and solace.[6] Not all were political in nature, but those with such a slant were prime carriers of revolutionary agitation, overwhelmingly liberal, and unabashedly propagandistic:

> To fan the patriotic flame,
> To cherish the desire of same,
> To bid the Irish youth aspire,
> To emulate the noble fire,
> Which dissipates the tyrant's bands,
> And Freedom gives to injur'd lands.
> . . . .
> Dear countrymen, these are our aims.[7]

For purposes of analysis these songs should be divided into four groups, although these types are not discrete and mutually exclusive: (1) general comments on the rights of man, freedom, rebellion, (2) comments on Paine, (3) comments on Burke, (4) comments on Paine-Burke together.

I

Ireland had identified her cause with that of America from the first rumblings of political dissatisfaction in that distant land. Both countries had long chafed under colonial status. Many Irish had emigrated to America, and their bond of brotherhood with those still in the old country was strong: they were bound by what Francis Lieber called of a later period "the strong tie of bearing one common wrong." After America's successful rebellion the Irish, from the misery of their own land, sang of the New World with longing and hope:

> America! thou lovely nation,
> 　Offspring of eternal day,
> Shall not the whole creation
> 　Homage to thy virtue pay.
> 　　Viva la! long live the People,
> 　　Viva la! the Rights of Man,
> 　　Viva la! America,
> 　　It was in you it first began.[8]

Increasingly through the years the Irish realized that to be successful against the English they had to be united behind the common goal. So numerous songs exhorted the various factions to subordinate their petty differences to the greater good. Religious differences especially should be subordinated. One popular broadside ballad was entitled "The Rights of Man." In it the author dreams of seeing St. Patrick descend from heaven and pray that the Catholics, Presbyterians, and other Protestants unite against the general enemy:

> He says, I'll lead you, and always aid you,
> Let none subdue it, its three in one,
> To prove the unity of that community,
> That holds in lenity the rights of man.[9]

France, like America, came to symbolize freedom, and such a dramatic event as the fall of the Bastille was applauded in songs like the following, "The Glorious Exertion of Man. 14th July, 1789":

> Gallia burst her vile shackles on this glorious day,
> 　And we dare to applaud the great deed:
> We dare to exult in a tyrant's lost sway,
> 　And rejoice that a nation is freed:

For this we assemble, regardless of those
    Who wish to enslave the free mind:
Our foes we are conscious, are liberty's foes
And our friends are the friends of Mankind.[10]

Witnessing the success of the Americans and French in achieving their goals, the Irish demanded their "natural rights":

Tell ribbands, crowns and stars,
    Kings, traitors, troops and wars,
Plans, councils, plots and jars,
    We will be free.
God save "The Rights of Man," etc. [sic].[11]

God-given rights assisted by reason assured the Irish of eventual freedom. But to forestall liberty, the English masters had been forced to outlaw reason, as one bitterly ironic song chronicles: It is not the people but principle that threatens the throne. On all sides it advances. The only way to save the kingdom from overthrow therefore is to "darken the mind":

Let the press be confin'd,
A law against reading and speaking:
    Such bondage must pass,
    Among every class.
And let it be called their own seeking.
    And next to secure,
    Their loyalty sure,
Let Thinking be deem'd high-treason;
    For still after all,
    Our system must fall,
Unless we are lords of their Reason. (*Resource* I, 55-56)

II

In many songs Paine's name and teachings were called upon in a general way to stir up active rebellion. One, for example, stated: "Remember Thomas Paine!/His arguments point out the way/Your Freedom to regain." (*Harp*, pp. 26-27) Another more definitely outlined the cure for malignant slavery:

Brave Irish no longer inactive remain,
    Attend to the dictates of Reason and Paine;
'Tis to Freedom they call you, no longer delay,
    Your rights are at stake, and are lost if you stay.[12]

Another piece, gaining prestige by its epic sweep, disdains to touch on the bloody battles of old as being irrelevant, but turns instead to the subject of Freedom. Although Freedom "long had dormant lain," it now "deigns to visit Man again." The prime mover in its re-introduction is Paine, the only person named in the song, and its documents Paine's works:

And first that brave unrival'd chief,
  Who did her cause maintain,
Whose work evinc'd in every leaf,
  Their godlike author, Paine.

. . . .

A bolder champion to engage,
  Falsehood had ne'er found;
Resplendent Truth illum'd each page,
  And flash'd conviction round.[13]

Arthur O'Connor, the fiery Irish patriot, wrote "verses" which he "distributed" "on his way to confinement in Fort George, in Scotland, 1798," as the headnote to the work explains, and which were reprinted in the songbooks, though apparently never sung. Because of the unusual presentation of this work, I reproduce all of it, plus the note:

The pomp of courts and pride of kings,
I prize above all earthly things;
I love my country; but the king,
Above all men his praise I sing:
The royal banners are display'd,
And may success the standard aid.

I fain would banish far from hence,
The Rights of Man and Common Sense;
Confusion to his odious reign,
That foe to princes, Thomas Paine!
Defeat and ruin seize the cause
Of France, its liberties, and laws!

Nothing objectionable is here obvious to the reader; but to learn the real sentiments of the writer, the first line of the first verse must be taken, and next the first line of the second, the second line of the first and second line of the second, and so on alternately.[14]

One of the most curious songs in these books of generally serious propaganda is a piece entitled "The Hearty Fellow's Deligt" [sic]. A drinking song, it is significant in revealing how thoroughly radical sentiments permeated everyday Irish life. It is important also in being apparently the first public coupling of Paine's name with drinking. Though the purpose of the song is to demonstrate the stimulating power of drink—even the great Thomas Paine's genius was improved by it—it may have planted a seed in the minds of people which made them receptive later to charges against Paine of inebriety:

The mighty Thomas Paine,
  Who freedom did maintain,
With energy of reason and sense,
  Was stupid as an ass,

Till first he took a glass,
Then truth sprung from his cruskeen lan. (*Resource* I, 23)

Paine's two most inflammatory political works, *Common Sense* (1776) and *Rights of Man* (1791-92), were more completely exploited than is evidenced in the preceding excerpts. The thesis of the earlier publication became one of the most widespread of the propagandistic songs, in what was essentially a simplified version of the original. I quote the whole piece:

> Common Sense
> (Tune—"Girl I Left Behind Me.")
> Oh why should weak deluded man,
>   So long continue blind, sir?
> Why should he raise a fancied form,
>   To impose upon his mind, sir?
> When all appear of equal worth
>   Before the eye of Heaven;
> Why should he idly dread that power
>   Which he himself has given?
>
> Why should he tamely bow to those
>   Who class him with the swine, sir,
> Who bid him eat his bitter bread,
>   Nor offer to repine, sir?
> Who dare alas, with shameless front,
>   Assert that 'twould do good, sir,
> If e'er he murmur forth his wrongs,
>   To silence them with blood, sir.
>
> Why should the gewgaw tricks of state,
>   Impose upon his reason?
> Such toys and play things are but fit
>   For childhood's simple season.
> The jewels sparkling on the breast,
>   A *child's* regard may win, sir.
> The manly mind looks not for these,
>   But asks the gem within, sir.
>
> Man wants no ornament of state,
>   No trick to make him greater,
> The pompous vestments but deface
>   The image of his maker;
> The simple garb and plain attire
>   The honest heart best suit, sir.
> For *virtue* only makes the *man*
>   Superior to the *brute,* sir. (*Resource I,* 63)

Paine's later and more immediate work widely stimulated songs. One piece commented on the futile efforts of the English government to suppress Paine, as was attempted when word of the *Rights* reached the ears of Government:

> The bold *Rights of Man* struck such terror and fear
> That stern proclamations in all parts appear,
> But deter us they can't—for as Friends we'll agree,
> The state to reform—and we'll die or be free.   (*Harp*, pp. 25-26)

Another song is a virtual setting to music of Paine's arguments. This, too, demands publication in its entirety:

The Divine Right of the Majesty of the People

> When first the Almighty form'd the world
> And peopled thick the fertile Ball,
> His sacred banner he unfurl'd,
> And Liberty, dear Liberty! proclaimed to all.

> He gave no King, no King tyrannic sway.
> In chains he bade no captives groan:
> He bade not millions one obey,
> Nor made that gaudy Toy a crown.

> The beasts in Freedom rang'd the grove,
> Unceas'd the warblers cut the air;
> For all was harmony and love,
> Since Liberty, sweet nymph, was there.

> Not then, not then the ruffian shield and spear,
> Encircl'd the usurper's throne:
> Man's equal Rights each man held dear,
> For justice, equal justice rul'd alone.

> Men, you were equal made by Heaven,
> Your equal birthright Liberty;
> Dare to assert the boon thus giv'n,
> Since Heaven commands you to be Free.

> Should tyrants e'er your Rights invade,
> Crush at a blow the serpent brood;
> Upon his neck indignant tread,
> And sound your Freedom in their blood.   (*Harp*, pp. 12-13)

Another piece, this time the opposite side of the coin, was widely used to energize rebellion. Entitled "The Rights of Man," written "By His Lordship," it enumerates in exaggerated terms what royalists think the commoner's rights are, as this excerpt demonstrates:

> Kings have a right divine to be
>   Your Lords, and Gods and masters;
> And commons, peers, and priests agree,
>   To laugh at your disasters.

> You have a right to all the toil,
> You have a right to chain your tongue,
> You have a right to live and breathe,
> You have a right to wear your rags.

>   Chorus
> For kings and lords, the Rights of Man
>   Were first of all intended;
> And since the reign of kings began,
>   The Rights of Man are ended.[15]

III

In his attack on republicanism in France—and throughout the world—Burke fell victim to his love of rhetoric, a love which in his later years in Commons caused him to be called "Dinner Bell," because when he began to speak, regardless of the hour the other members went to dinner. And he stated in unfortunate words doctrines which had they been less extravagantly voiced might have been more temperately received. Popularizers must always break up long literary works, seizing upon significant or quotable material in their effort to make the authors remembered by the people. Thus were hung around Burke's neck albatrosses he could not shake off.

One of Burke's most haunting ghosts was his gloomy forecast of the decline of learning in a republic: "Along with its natural protectors and guardians, learning will be cast into the mire, and trodden under the hoofs of a swinish multitude," he predicted. The unfortunate term "swinish multitude" stuck. Everyone used it, the conservative with approbation, the insulted with deep resentment. Burke's name did not have to be attached to it in any way for it to be immediately identifiable. Songs of attack blossomed. One book containing some eighty songs was entitled *A Tribute to the Swinish Multitude*. Published first in London, it was reprinted in New York in 1795 and was known in Ireland; the songs it contained were widely sung there, with adaptations to local circumstances.

In a long introduction the editor attacks Burke and his royalist ilk. Burke is an "apostate courtier, who has dared, in the full spirit of his impudence, to call the majority and support of the nation, a "Swinish multitude.'" One of the most important and widespread songs in this book is "Burke's Address to the 'Swinish Multitude.'" (tune: "Derry down, down") Though written in England, it took deep root in Irish soil, with appropriate alterations. I quote seven of its twelve heavily ironic stanzas:

> Ye vile Swinish herd, in the stye of taxation,
> What would ye be after disturbing the nation?
> Give over your grunting—be off—to your stye!
> Nor dare to look out, if a King passes by:
> Get ye down, down—down, keep ye down!

> Do you know what a king is? By Patrick I'll tell ye;
> He has power in his pocket to buy you and sell you;
> To make you his soldiers or keep you at work;
> To hang you, and cure you, for ham or salt pork!

Do you think that a king is no more than a man?
Ye Irish, ye swinish ironical clan!
I swear by his office, his right is divine,
To flog you, and feed you, and treat you like swine.

Now the church and the state, to keep each other warm,
Are married together. And where is the harm?
How healthy and wealthy are husband and wife!
But swine are excluded the conjugal life—

The state, it is true, has grown fat upon Swine,
The church's weak stomach on Tythe-pig can dine;
But neither you know, as they roast by the fire!
Have a right to find fault with the cooks, or enquire.
. . . .

Here's myself, and his darkness, and Harry Dund-ass;
Scotch, English, and Irish, with fronts made of brass—
A cord plated three-fold will stand a good pull,
Against Sawney, and Patrick and old Johnny Bull!!!

To conclude, then, no more about Man and his Rights,
Tom Paine, and a rabble of Liberty-lights;
That you are but our "SWINE," if you ever forget,
We'll throw you alive to the horrible PITT!
        Get ye down.[16]

Numerous other songs incorporated Burke's reference to the
"swine" into related or generally unrelated matter. One, for
example, which is crying out against war with France, as Burke
demanded, says:

The swine, as Burke calls them, did grunt and did groan;
"No war," they cried out with pitiful tone.[17]

One ironically summons up Biblical defense for Burke:

As it was forbid by an ancient divine
    To throw precious pearls to ignorant swine;
Complying with this, my ambition should be
    To keep them still bond slaves, ourselves being free.[18]

Another calls upon those men who would rise from their supine
misery and if necessary die for freedom, who:

By Bastiles ne'er appall'd
See Nature's Rights renew'd,
No longer unaveng'd be called
    "The Swinish Multitude."   (Harp, pp. 51-52)

One asserts that since it is forbidden for the People to "sing of the
Rights of Mankind," "as swine, let's assemble to grunt out our
wrongs" (Resource I, 61-62). In another:

I said to old Burke, for d'ye see he would cry,
    When France had resolv'd to be free:
What argufy's (sic) grunting like hogs in a stye,
    Why what a blind fool you must be;
. . . .
And if to the *lanterne* you go my friend Burke,
    We never shall be plagued with you more. (*Resource I*, 53-54)

Yet another uses Burke's reference, in looking to France as the guardian of the hated People:

From France now see Liberty's Tree,
    Its branches wide extending;
The swine to it for shelter run—
    Full fast they are assembling.

They grunt and groan with ludicrous tone,
    Against all base connivers,
They now unite and swear they'll bite
    Their most unfeeling drivers. (*Resource II*, 6)

Burke was surely one of the most misunderstood men who ever lived. His apparent about-face in political principles from approval of the American revolution to violent condemnation of the same movement in France was both inexplicable and dismaying to many. Many felt that the switch was a crass sellout, that Burke was secretly a pensioner. Paine, for example, continually reproved his adversary for being a kept propagandist. That he was innocent of the charge—that he was not receiving any pension, and that his change in political position was a natural outgrowth of his deep-seated belief in conservative order and an awesome respect for Britain's government—in no wise mollified people's ire. The common men's hatred and contempt were intense, as the following excerpt illustrates:

APOSTATE! give over your eloquence, pray,
No more on the subject of Monarchy say:
Exalted in office, and fed by the Swine—
If we should desert you, you'll catch a decline.
    Tumble down, down—down—down—come ye down.

But we cannot well brook to be called the Swine.
Let man have his Rights, and the epithet's thine;
Apostate thou art—and allur'd by the hire,
Return like a few that was wash'd—to the mire.

Our thanks we set—you may think it a joke,
For the blessed enquiry your writings provoke;
We thank you for thwarting your own bad design;
The bacon and pork are restor'd to the swine. (*Tribute*, pp. 43-45)

Numerous other songs were sung to the tune of the original piece. So Burke's vivid phrase became the most widely used club with which his opponents beat him.

One quite sophisticated piece glories in France's "day-star of liberty," "an effulgence so mild, with a lustre so bright," then turns to Burke:

> Let Burke, like a bat, from its splendor retire,
>   A splendor too strong for his eyes;
> Let pedants and fools his effusions admire,
>   Intrapt in his cobwebs, like flies:
> Shall phrenzy, and sophistry hope to prevail,
>   Where reason opposes her weight?   (*Resource I*, 20-21)

Appropriately the tune of this song is that of Paine's "The Death of General Wolfe," a piece which he originally wrote to be sung at the Headstrong Club of Lewes, England, and which was first published with music in the *Pennsylvania Magazine*, March, 1775.[19]

One of the most effective blows delivered against Burke resulted from his highly emotional and foolish idolatry of the French Queen, an attitude which one critic of the *Reflections* called "pure foppery," but which Burke persisted in defending.[20] The editor of the *Tribute to the Swinish Multitude* quoted Burke's passage at great length as the introduction to an attacking song, interspersing his own comments in a "Key," as this brief passage, with the "Key" in brackets, demonstrates (pp. 20-21):

> It is now sixteen or seventeen years since I saw the queen of France, then the Dauphiness, at Versailles; and surely [says he, speaking of the last Queen of France] never lighted this orb, which she hardly seemed to touch, a more delightful vision. . . . Little did I dream that I should have lived to see such disasters fallen upon her in a nation of gallant men, in a nation of men of honor, and cavaliers!   I thought ten thousand swords must have leaped from their scabbards to avenge [what] even a look that threatened her with insult.

Then the editor comments:

> Surely, Reader, if you possess one grain of common sense, you will say that either this passage is not quoted from Burke's celebrated Defence of Royalty, or that the author took leave of his senses when he wrote it.—I have looked into his book three times, that I might not mistake, and I am willing to make affidavit that you may find it in page 112.

Then follow songs which ironically and rather artistically out-Burke the master. I quote one at length (pp. 25-26):

>   Plaintive
> I saw, but O I surely dream'd
> A vision dropt from heaven (it seem'd);

The world a brighter lustre wore,
Than ever man beheld before.

Philosophers could not declare
Which powers did most attraction share;
If to the vision, earth arose,
Or—descended—no one knows.

Ten thousand Dons and Cavaliers
Around her stand with swords and spears,
To be her slaves was all they sought,
Thus was "The grace of life unbought."
. . . .
But, O! how Time's revolving glass
Brings unexpected things to pass!
The Queen is driven from her throne,
The Age of Chivalry is gone!
. . . .
Come kingly butchers, then, advance,
And desolate the plains of France;
Alas! ye move but slowly on!
The Age of Chivalry is gone!

Then bring my Rosinante, that I
My prowess in the field may try;
It would reward my toil and pain,
Could I restore that AGE again.

But, ah!—No more—I will not go,
REASON appears my potent foe;
'Tis REASON keeps her from the throne,
The Age of Chivalry is gone.

IV

In this controversy usually the singers, perhaps for the sake of simplicity, kept the combatants separated. There were, as the above quotations indicate, instances when Paine had to be squared off against Burke to show the absurdity or the weakness of the latter or the superiority of the former. But such instances were in the minority. There were few full-scale engagements in which the two political philosophers met, and before the very eyes, as it were, of the singers, right-thinking triumphed over wrong-thinking. There is one piece, however, in which just this occurs. It is an epic tourney between Burke and Paine, a real battle of the books, which in its approach, mood, humor and outcome actually recapitulates the whole controversy and the age in which it occurred.

Song
(Tune: *Chevy Chace*)

They prosper best who have no king
    To rob them and enthrall;
Then let our acclamations ring
    At ev'ry tyrant's fall.

To drive the despots from their throne
    And statesmen from their place:
A woeful fighting is begun
    Among the human race.

Now Edmund Burke, a rueful knight,
    (Whose tender heart did ache
To see the people gain their Right)
    A solemn vow did make,

That paper-pen—and eke ink-horn,
    Should put them to the rout;
The child shall bless that is unborn,
    The writings he sent out.*
His thoughts with phrase theatric clad,
    Were strong to melt the ear;
And metaphoric speech he had
    To make his subject clear.

With LOYALTY his bosom glowed
    And as he lov'd the gold;
A little pension21 was bestow'd
    To make his fight more bold.

The rules of errantry he knew,
    And did to France repair;
To bid his peerless Queen adieu!
    And thus address'd the fair:
"Delightful vision! it is mete
    Thy blessing ere I go!
I'll soon return and at thy feet,
    Lay all my conquests low!"

She smiled—when turning quickly found,
    He vanish'd from her sight;
And like a hero took his ground,
    Already for the fight.—

These tidings came to Thomas Paine,
    A man of courage bold;
Who could the "Rights of man" explain
    And King-craft too unfold.

* (*That is, for the Enquiry they have provoked.*)

With heart and head both sound and clear,
    The course he undertook;
And now in battle both appear,
    And Book appears to Book.

Loud vaunted Edmund in the field,
    Like Quixote 'mongst the sheep;
Who thought with such a sword and shield
    To end them at a sweep!

The valour of Sir Knight was great,
    For in his rear we find;
To cover, if he should retreat,
    Were but a FEW inclined.

While Paine (the foe of kings) appears
    Majestic on the plain;
The shout of ALL THE WORLD he hears,
    And sees them in his train!

With courage did the knight advance,
    Discerning not his foe;
He challeng'd all the knights of France,
    And aim'd the dreadful blow!

He gave them warning to retreat
    And wondered at their stay;
He little thought so soon to meet
    Obstruction in his way.

A thousand paces back he ran,
    At sight of warlike Paine;
And soon were seen THE RIGHTS OF MAN
    Triumphant on the plain.

Base-born plebeian, said the knight,
    As he retired with speed;
It is not lawful we should fight
    With men of vulgar breed—

So saying, and all out of breath,
    Quick out of sight he steals;
And thought each moment cruel death
    Would seize his heavy heels.

These tidings came to George our king
    In Windsor where he lay—
What! What! what news, news do you bring,
    Has Edmund lost the day?

O, heavy, heavy news, he said!
    England can witness be,
There's none can give a monarch aid,
    Of such accounts as he.

The courts in black may all be hung,
    If they pursue the fight;
Our passing bell will soon be rung,
    If men obtain their right.

The victory was soon proclaim'd
    And eke the Monarch's dread;
Forbidding books all left unnam'd;
    Even to be sold or read.

At which the Presses aiming well,
    Full charged, they all let fly;
Enough was found the books to sell,
    Enough the books to buy.

And now the people will rejoice,
    Such tidings heard they never;
They cry aloud with cheerful voice,
    The RIGHTS OF MAN FOREVER!   (*Tribute*, pp. 29-33)

From the evidence one must inevitably conclude that revolutionary agitation in these songs in Ireland was strongly and noisily against Burke personally and against everything he advocated, and that it fed on the inspiration of Paine's works and on the example of the man himself. The question which naturally arises is, What were the results of all this expression of feeling and effort to propagandize? The answer is both complex and intangible.

That the Irish were in those days enthusiastic singers, as they have always been, goes without saying. There were hundreds, perhaps several thousand, ballads and songs sung in that country expressing the sentiments of the American Rebellion and the French Revolution and celebrating their dramatic happenings. That songs do strongly influence and motivate behavior also goes without challenge. One conservative editor of a book of songs half a generation after our period commented on the "magical effects" of the song "Lillibullero" in the rebellion of the English against the "Biggoted and Tyrannical Government of James the Second," of the "dreadful influence of 'Ca Ira' in the French Revolution, and 'Erin Go Brach' in the Irish Rebellion of 1798."[22] If he had been attempting a full catalogue of such songs undoubtedly he would have included some of those given in this paper.

For these songs formed yet another bond between the nationalists and revolutionists of all ranks and levels of poverty or wealth. The lyrics were of sufficient literary merit to make them palatable to persons other than the poor and ignorant. In fact, they were written wholly or largely by the educated: the diction, figures of speech, flights of fancy, the polish—all indicate authorship by the literate. Yet they were simple enough to be understood, appreciated, cherished by the humblest. Thus the poor, naked and starving, who had only their wrath to warm them, their spiritual nourishment to sustain them, found both lavishly provided in these songs. These people joined revolutionary organizations—for example, the United Irishmen, which was founded in 1791 and which exploded the rebellion of 1798. The leaders of these United Irishmen, as well as other revolutionists—W. P. McCabe, Wolfe Tone, Edward Fitzgerald, Thomas A. Emmet, and more—knew that the peasantry, fired by these songs, could be relied upon for manpower.

Notes

[1] *Freeman's Journal, Dublin Journal, Dublin Chronicle.* Quoted in R. B. McDowell, *Irish Public Opinion, 1750-1800* (London, Faber and Faber, 1944), p. 164.

[2] *Hibernian Journal, Dublin Weekly Journal, Morning Post, Bedfast News Letter.* Quoted in McDowell, *Irish Public Opinion,* p. 164.

[3] For examples see *ibid.* The Burke-Paine controversy divided and inflamed the nation. Political clubs sprang up everywhere. Tracts, ballads, pamphlets, broadsides poured from the Irish presses. One contemporary observer wrote: "The merchant dispatched them as the packages of his wares, the countrymen received them inclosing his snuff and tobacco; they were scattered along the roads to meet accidental readers and they were left in parcels at the doors of the peasantry." Another contemporary wrote to a friend in France in 1791: "The impression which Paine's *Rights of Man* has made in Ireland is, I am informed, hardly to be conceived." Both quotes in Richard Hayes, *Ireland and Irishmen in the French Revolution* (London: E. Benn, 1932), p. 8. La Luzerne, French Minister at London, reported that twenty-five thousand copies had been printed by the republican clubs to be sold at minimal prices or given away throughout the remotest places of England and Ireland (A. O. Aldridge, *Man of Reason* [Philadelphia: Lippincott, pp. 142-43]). In the *Morning Chronicle,* 24 July 1784, there appeared a letter by Burke in which he commented on the "extravagant courses" then being adopted in Ireland. "Everything is running to some desperate extremity . . . & despotism is only to be cured by popular Phrenzy." A toast popular at this time was: "The British Army, and may the French never overtake them!" (See Thomas H. D. Mahoney, *Edmund Burke and Ireland,* [Cambridge, Mass.: Harvard University Press, 1960, p. 222.])

4 The *Cork Gazette,* a liberal paper, declared that Paine's "zeal for the dignity of the God Head and his indication of his divine and moral attributes are worthy of our admiration," and did not recant. The *Northern Star,* however, another liberal sheet, at first felt the *Age of Reason* as effective as any of Paine's other works; six months later it was glad to have refutations appear. The *Belfast News* was unfavorable from the beginning. These and the following citations are from McDowell, *Irish Public Opinion,* pp. 164-178.

5 Mahoney, however (pp. 139-40), mentions that Burke's love of verbosity and his apparent leanings toward the Jesuits made him the subject of numerous caricatures; in one he was pictured as being a follower of Satan (Fox). Also Mahoney quotes one ballad against Fox, part of which addresses Burke:

> For thee, *O beauteous and sublime!*
> What place of honour shall we find?
> To tempt with money were a crime;
> Thine are the riches of the mind.

> Clad in a matron's cap and robe,
> Thou shall assist each *wither'd crone!*
> And, as the piercing threat shall probe,
> Be't thine to lead the choral grone! (*sic*)

> Thine to uplift the whiten'd eye,
> And thine to spread th' uplifted hand!
> Thine to upheave th' expressive sigh,
> And regulate the hoary band!

For a general, and thin, study see Patrick Galvin, *Irish Songs of Resistance* (New York: Folklore Press, 1955), which mentions neither Paine nor Burke.

6 According to A. L. Lloyd, noted British musicologist and folklorist, "The Rights of Man" is a very famous fiddle tune in Britain today.

7 *Paddy's Resource; or the Harp of Erin Attuned to Freedom. Being a Collection of Patriotic Songs; Selected for Paddy's Amusement* (Dublin: n.p., 1798), the Preface, hereafter cited as *Harp* (copy in Boston Public Library).

8 *Paddy's Resource. Being a Select Collection of Original and Modern Patriotic Songs, Toasts and Sentiments.* Compiled for the Use of all firm Patriots. First American edition (Philadelphia: T. Stephens, 1796), p. 59, hereafter cited as *Resource I* (copy in Library of Congress). For the quote see Carl Wittke, *The Irish in America* (Baton Rouge: Louisiana State University Press, 1956), p. 150.

9 In the Bradshaw Irish Collection, Cambridge University.

10 *Resource I,* 66. The tune was "General Wolfe," no doubt the same as that of Paine's song "The Death of General Wolfe," for which see below.

11 *Resource I,* 8. The tune was "Ca Ira," that of the most famous revolutionary song in France, and which was widely sung in Britain and America.

12 *Resource I*, 57. Also in *Tribute to the Swinish Multitude: Being a Choice Collection of Patriotic Songs.* Collected by the Celebrated R. Thomson (Philadelphia: Mathew Carey, 1796), p. 66, hereafter cited as *Tribute* (copy in Library of Congress).

13 *Harp,* pp. 32-33; *Resource I,* 58.

14 *The American Republican Harmonist; or a Collection of Songs, and Odes;* written in America, on American subjects and Principles: a Great number of them never before published (Philadelphia: William Duane, No. 106 High-Street, 1803), p. 130. Despite the declaration in the title, much of the material in this book was imported. (Copy in Library of Congress.)

15 *Harp,* pp. 40-42; *Tribute,* pp. 67-68.

16 Also in *Resource I,* 43; *Harp,* pp. 39-40. A different song with the same title appeared in *Harp,* pp. 51-52; the tune is in *Harp,* pp. 14-15; the tune was also in the second edition of: *Paddy's Resource. Being a Select Collection of Original and Modern Patriotic Songs, Toasts and Sentiments.* From the latest Edition—with Corrections (New York: R. Wilson, 149 Pearl-Street; at the Request of a number of Hibernians in this Country, who were desirous of having copies of them, 1798), p. 4, hereafter cited as *Resource II.* (The only known extant copy of this songster is an incomplete one at the American Antiquarian Society.)

17 *Harp,* pp. 64-65; *Resource II,* 20.

18 *Resource I,* 16-17; *Resource II,* 25-27.

19 *The Complete Writings of Thomas Paine,* ed. Philip S. Foner (New York: Citadel Press, 1945), II, 1083.

20 In answer to this criticism of the *Reflections* by Philip Francis, Burke replied: "I tell you again,—that the recollection of the manner in which I saw the queen of France, in the year 1774, and the contrast . . . *did* draw tears from me and wetted my paper." Quoted in Alfred Cobban, *Edmund Burke and the Revolt Against the Eighteenth Century* (2nd ed. New York: Barnes and Noble, 1960), p. 121.

21 Throughout his political life Burke was plagued with the accusation that he was bought and kept by a pension. He was in fact always poverty stricken and careless in use of money. Also he unwisely associated himself with bills and with people whose actions cast some doubt on his fiscal integrity. Furthermore, he was always forced to seek loans from his rich political sponsors and allies. But he never in reality received any pensions until the last two years of his life. On August 30, 1794 Pitt wrote to him that the King had granted him a Civil List pension for £1200 for the life of himself and of his wife. The next year he got an additional £2500. Thus, in all, his pensions amounted to £3700. See Philip Magnus, *Edmund Burke: A Life* (London: John Murray, 1939), pp. 270-71.

22 *The Patriotic Songster; Containing a Choice Collection of Most Admired Loyal, Patriotic, and Constitutional Songs* (Strabane: Joseph Alexander, 1815), p. 1 (copy in British Museum). In America one need remember only such effective songs as "Yankee Doodle," "Dixie," "Over There," etc.

The Irish Short Story and Oral Tradition

Vivian Mercier

In discussing the Irish short story—by which I mean the short story as written in English, not Gaelic, by Irishmen—I start with two basic assumptions: first, that the Irish are particularly gifted for this genre; second, that they are paradoxically weak in the novel. These assumptions possess not the slightest originality; if they did, I should not be justified in treating them as axiomatic. Students and friends sometimes phrase them as questions: "why are the Irish so good at the short story?" "Why, James Joyce always excepted, are there so few good Irish novelists?" Before attempting to answer these questions, I might point out one indisputable fact: contemporary Irish writers almost never achieve success in both forms. In compiling a paperback anthology of Irish short stories, I decided to deviate from the "one author, one story" formula. There were five living authors whom I thought worthy of being represented by two stories each—Frank O'Connor, Liam O'Flaherty, Mary Lavin, Sean O'Faolain, and the 85-year-old Daniel Corkery. As I was compiling the biographical notices of these five, I observed a pattern: each of them had begun by publishing both a novel and a book of short stories within the first two or at most three years of his writing career, but sooner or later all ceased to write novels: Corkery after one, O'Connor and Miss Lavin after two, O'Faolain after three, and O'Flaherty after no fewer than fourteen, the last of which appeared in 1951, since when he has continued to publish short stories in both English and Gaelic. Mary Lavin, in the preface to her *Selected Stories,* went so far as to write, "I . . . wish that I could break up the two long novels I have published into the few short stories they ought to have been in the first place."[1] Much as I admire Frank O'Connor's second novel, *Dutch Interior* (1941), I must admit that it also disintegrates into a series of short stories when examined critically.

If we omit Elizabeth Bowen because she has written so little about Ireland and Irish people, it becomes impossible to present five living Irish novelists of a stature comparable with our short-story quintet's. Kate O'Brien, Francis Stuart, Brendan Kiely,

Brian Moore, Michael McLaverty—I list the names with diffidence, especially as McLaverty has published a single book of short stories which far outshines any of his novels that I have read. Setting Joyce and George Moore in a separate category, we can generalize about the main body of Irish fiction writers to the effect that they are more likely to attain mastery in the short story than in the novel and, if they do master the shorter form are prone to give up the novel altogether. Furthermore, we cannot attribute this emerging pattern to commercial influences, for it is a truism that a volume of short stories, even if each story has appeared in one of the better-paying magazines beforehand, cannot earn its author wealth or contemporary fame on a scale at all comparable with that attainable by a best-selling novel.

Having somewhat confirmed the validity of my two assumptions, we can go on to another question—Is contemporary Irish fiction closer to oral literature than, say, contemporary English fiction is? There seems only one possible answer: "Yes, of course!" Will this, then, explain at one stroke both Irish skill in the shorter form and Irish incompetence in the longer one? I think so, but we shall have to examine carefully just what we mean by "closer" in the phrase "closer to oral literature"; indeed, I shall have to present a careful definition of "oral literature."

Let us first, however, note the ambiguity of "closer": Irish fiction may be close to oral literature in at least two different ways. On the one hand, it may present many of the characteristics of oral literature without having been directly influenced by it— an improbable but not impossible coincidence. Or it may have been directly influenced by oral literature. I favor the latter view, but the complexity and incompleteness of the influence will have to be gone into at considerable length.

The argument in favor of mere coincidence can be dealt with more briefly, but it cannot be dismissed as altogether frivolous. Irish fiction in English does not begin with Swift or Goldsmith or Henry Brooke, none of whom dealt specifically with Irish scenes and character, though all had spent their formative years in Ireland. By coincidence or not, Irish fiction begins with *Castle Rackrent,* in which the history of the Rackrent family is told by their faithful servant, Thady Quirk; I say "told" advisedly, for Thady's memoir, though supposedly written down by him, is full of the rhythm and idiom of the spoken language. Neither the rhythm nor most of the idiom is distinctively Irish, but this seems to have been the first attempt in English since Elizabethan days to write a fairly lengthy narrative—30,000 words—entirely in oral style. Such a style had been used latterly in brief, humorous sketches and poems like Swift's "Mrs. Frances Harris's Petition," whereas *Castle Rackrent* is distinguished by its length and occasional seriousness. The following passage will serve to refresh our memories of the style—not too different perhaps, from that of Fielding's landladies—and to illustrate its adaptation to a serious mood:

> There was then a great silence in Castle Rackrent, and I went moping from room to room, hearing the doors clap for want of right locks, and the wind through the broken windows, that the glazier never would come to mend, and the rain coming through the roof and best ceilings all over the house for want of the slater, whose bill was not paid, besides our having no slates or shingles for that part of the old building which was shingled and burnt when the chimney took fire, and had been open to the weather ever since.

Once Maria Edgeworth had shown that the thing could be done, it was done over and over again by others who had a far better command of Irish English than the originator. She herself, I believe, never employed the technique again except in brief passages, and none of her successors in nineteenth-century Ireland exploited the opportunities for irony that she had shown the style to possess. It was left for Mark Twain to grasp those opportunities anew in another country.

Castle Rackrent has little in common with true oral literature—i.e., folklore—except the fact that it employs the spoken language; it is oral as *Huckleberry Finn* is oral, or Ring Lardner, or much of Faulkner. One could argue very reasonably that *Castle Rackrent* sprang from nothing but Maria Edgeworth's fascination with "the brogue" and with the oddities of Irish life and character as they had first impinged upon her at the age of fifteen after her upbringing in England. Ireland must have seemed theatrical and a little unreal to the impressionable girl, just as the great Anglo-Irish dramatists, traveling in the opposite direction during their teens and very early twenties, were unable to see London and English life generally as anything but a comedy—which, sooner or later, they would but in its proper perspective upon the stage.

It would be reasonable, too, to argue that the fiction writers of Gaelic stock who followed where Maria had led the way were indifferent to the oral tradition and adopted the brogue for a variety of practical and even aesthetic reasons. In the first place, the brogue had been popular on the stage all through the eighteenth century, and even earlier than that.[2] Miss Edgeworth and Lady Morgan had shown that it could be equally popular in the novel —not to mention the fabulous acclaim which Sir Walter Scott had earned by taking his cue from *Castle Rackrent,* as he generously admitted, and exploiting the Scots vernacular. In the second place, the realistic convention of the novel virtually demanded that the brogue should be faithfully rendered in dialogue. Finally, there was an over-riding aesthetic consideration which William Carleton consciously recognized, though Gerald Griffin and John and Michael Banim may have grasped it only instinctively: lacking in education and social status as they all were in varying degrees, they did not write standard English with upper-class assurance and grace. In fact, the hack work that Griffin and John Banim had slaved at in London made them prone to cockney journalese, while the written English that Carleton learned in hedge schools and from the Dublin newspapers was certainly no better than theirs; the only living English that these four writers knew was the brogue—the English powerfully influenced by Gaelic phonology, speech rhythm, syntax, and even vocabulary, that was spoken by the poorer classes in the Irish towns and countryside. At the risk of sounding class-conscious and even bigoted, one must insist that without an education at Trinity College, Dublin—and, alas, very often even with it—a nineteenth-century Irish writer could not escape the pseudo-gentility, condescending pomposity, and weak facetiousness of middle-class, provincial, journalistic English. The same is true of Scots writers who use standard English; unless they have attended one of the Scots universities, they descend very easily to the level of Burns's and Fergusson's insipid English poems. In spite of the fine qualities so judiciously praised by Thomas Flanagan in *The Irish Novelists 1800-1850,*[3] Irish fiction of that period and later will always repel many of us by the poor quality of its narrative and descriptive prose. I can stand the melodramatic incidents, the exaggerated stereotypes which often pass for characters, the manic gloom and the equally manic high spirits; what I cannot stand is the mentality and vocabulary of the ambitious shopkeeper or village schoolmaster who is narrating describing and moralizing upon the events and persons displayed. Much of our twentieth-century Irish fiction is still written by present and former village schoolmasters, but—thanks be to God and Flaubert—they keep themselves and the written English they inculcate in the classroom out of their creative work; at any rate, the good ones do.

But aside from these three important reasons for the employment of the brogue, there is irrefutable evidence for the direct influence of oral literature on Carleton and Griffin, since both these writers intersperse their original short stories with Irish adaptations of international folktales; and, naturally enough, it is in these tales that we sometimes find the narration and description as well as the dialogue given in the brogue. An example is "The Three Tasks," which appears very incongruously in Carleton's sternly realistic *Traits and Stories of the Irish Peasantry*. The title character in the story "Ned M'Keown" relates "The Three Tasks" with casual facetiousness which shows little respect for tradition, but Carleton almost certainly heard the story originally from a "shanachie" or traditional storyteller. Carleton's own father was such a storyteller, and an exceptionally gifted one:

> . . . his memory was a perfect storehouse, and a rich one, of all that the social antiquary, the man of letters, the poet, or the musician, would consider valuable. As a teller of old tales, legends, and historical anecdotes he was unrivalled, and his stock of them was inexhaustible. He spoke the Irish and English languages with nearly equal fluency.[4]

By this, as internal evidence shows, Carleton meant that his father's English was nearly as good as his Gaelic—whereas his mother's was not. Carleton goes on to assert that he "hardly ever since heard . . . any single tradition, usage, or legend, that . . . was perfectly new to me or unheard before, in some similar or cognate dress." He then reveals how correctly he valued this heritage from the viewpoint of style as well as subject matter:

> What rendered this besides of such peculiar advantage to me in after life, as a literary man, was, that I heard them as often in the Irish language as in the English, if not oftener: a circumstance which enabled me in my writings to transfer the genius, the idiomatic peculiarity and conversational spirit of the one language into the other, precisely as the people themselves do in their dialogue, whenever the heart or imagination happens to be moved by the darker or better passions.[5]

In one of his sketches for the *Irish Penny Journal*, "The Irish Shanahus," Carleton gives a less idealized picture of an Irish tradition-bearer, Tom Grassiey, or Tom the Shoemaker, whom he describes as a "humble old man who, feeling himself gifted with a strong memory for genealogical history, old family anecdotes, and legendary lore in general, passes a happy life in going from family to family. "Carleton shows him to possess a really formidable memory although or rather because, he was completely illiterate." This memory could become a hindrance as well as a help:

> His language, when he spoke Irish, was fluent, clear, and sometimes eloquent; but when he had recourse to the English, although his fluency remained, yet it was the fluency of a man who made an indiscriminate use of a vocabulary which he did not understand. His pedantry on this account was highly ludicrous and amusing, and his wit and humor surprisingly original and pointed.[6]

Perhaps this passage, which may apply also to Carleton's father, explains why Carleton's versions of folktales—told, of necessity, in English—are always full of pedantries and other absurdities of expression. We shall see later, however, that Gaelic folktales give special honor to obscure and archaic passages known as "runs."

Griffin may not have had as intimate a relationship with the oral tradition as Carleton did and seems to have known little or no Gaelic. On the other hand, he records folklore more carefully than did the older writer. "The Brown Man" in *Holland-Tide* (1827), his first book of short fiction, is a version of Aarne-Thompson Type 363, a story of a male vampire "almost entirely confined to the shores of the Baltic and to Norway" according to Stith Thompson.[7] Griffin doubtless collected it in Gaelic or English near his native Limerick, which is, after all, a city of Norse foundation and has had a trade with Scandinavia in much more recent times. I must add with chagrin that Griffin's facetiousness almost ruins this eerie tale through remarks like "It was a very fine morning in those parts, for it was only snowing and hailing"—unless, indeed, his oral source is to blame. Another folktale in the same volume, "Owney and Owney-na-Peak," receives more respectful treatment from Griffin; not only are many of the narrative passages given in the brogue, but the brogue itself is fairly free of pedantry and facetiousness. One motif in this story, Owney's overhearing in a graveyard the deliberations of a council of cats, including the King of the Cats himself, was previously familiar to me only in a Gaelic oral version that I had heard in class from a native speaker of Gaelic. Griffin's posthumous volume *Talis Qualis; or Tales of the Jury-Room* (1842) contains at least one elaborate folktale, "The Story-Teller at Fault," and an even more curious item in the shape of a translation from the Gaelic literary tradition, what may be the first published English version of *Oidheadh Clainne Lir (The Fate of the Children of Lir)*. Thomas Moore had versified the "Song of Fionnuala" from a manuscript translation, but the story of the four children changed into swans, which has since become widely known, had never, I think, been printed in full until Griffin's rather wooden version. However, the problem of the influence of the oral tradition is complicated enough without our adding to it that raised by the literary tradition.

There is no point in examining in detail the knowledge of the oral tradition displayed by each individual nineteenth-century Irish fiction writer: Carleton represents the maximum exposure to the tradition, both in Gaelic and English; Griffin stands on more typical middle ground; Charles Lever might represent the minimum. Alongside the creative writers like Griffin and Carleton who mingle folklore with original short stories, we must recognize the existence of collectors like T. Crofton Croker, a pioneer with his *Fairy Legends and Traditions of the South of Ireland* (1825), and Patrick Kennedy, who, in a story like "Cauth Morrisy Looking for Service," seems to record his English-speaking sources with striking fidelity.[8] On the other hand, Samuel Lover's folklore strikes me as often no more authentic than *The Ingoldsby Legends*. In fairness to Lover, we must remember that a great deal of what was once Gaelic folklore lingered on in English-speaking districts throughout the nineteenth century. Writing in 1945, Professor J. H. Delargy said that this persistence of Gaelic folktales in English was still signficant in certain areas of the country:

> Both the international as well as the native *märchen* are more generally to be found in Irish than in English, and although many folk-tales of this kind have been recorded in English, the Anglo-Irish wonder-tale of the international type compares very unfavourably both as to style and content with similar tales in Irish. I have known story-tellers in Clare who could tell folktales (*märchen*) in both Irish and English, but it was quite evident that they told them much better in the Irish language in which they had first heard them.[9]

When we turn from the nineteenth century to living writers, the relationship to the oral tradition still exists, but its character has changed, for since the foundation of the Gaelic League by Douglas Hyde in 1893, Irish writers have been living in the era of the Gaelic revival. Let us look at what this has meant to the five "living masters" cited earlier. Daniel Corkery learned his Irish from the Gaelic League and personally encouraged O'Faolain and O'Connor to learn it there too. O'Faolain must have improved his knowledge of the language at the National University, where Gaelic has been compulsory since 1909, while O'Connor tells us that he attained a really firm grip on the language in prison camp after the Irish Civil War of 1922-23.[10] Since the language revivalists have made almost a fetish of the spoken language (*cainnt na ndaoine,* meaning literally "The people's speech"), we can be certain that Corkery, O'Faolain, and O'Connor could not have escaped the oral tradition, supposing they had been foolish enough to want to. Mary Lavin, who is young enough to have had compulsory Irish both at school and at the National University, for that very reason probably knows less Gaelic and has had less contact (if any) with the oral tradition than any other member of our five. As for Liam O'Flaherty, he is a native speaker of Gaelic and therefore born into the oral tradition, but, paradoxically, he is also the least oral in his approach to narrative of all five writers. I agree with Frank O'Connor's statement that O'Flaherty's English "lacks the distinction and beauty of his Gaelic,"[11] but—even in Gaelic O'Flaherty writes far more for the eye than he does for the ear or the speaking voice. Why is this? One's first answer must refer to individual temperament: O'Flaherty writes as naturally for the eye as the mature Joyce wrote for the ear; it is no accident that *The Informer* provided the outline for one of the most admired films ever made in Hollywood. I could point to thousands of passages in O'Flaherty's novels and short stories which are seen through the eye of a camera; two notable examples occur to me at once, the murder scene in *The Assassin* and the short story called "The Landing," though every one of his animal stories is also conceived in cinematic terms.[12] O'Flaherty resembles no single writer so closely as he does the late great documentary film director Robert Flaherty, who filmed so many of his namesake's subjects in *Man of Aran.*

I would suggest a second reason, connected with the revival of Gaelic, to explain why O'Flaherty is so exempt from the influence of the oral tradition: he is *literate* in Gaelic, and doubtless has been so since his earliest years in elementary school. In contrast, Carleton was completely illiterate in Gaelic until the day he died; some of the phonetic equivalents for Gaelic phrases that he uses in his stories might well make a Celtic scholar weep. Whereas a Carleton, by his own avowal, is constantly transferring oral Gaelic into written English, an O'Flaherty may translate visual images directly into the written symbols of whichever language he happens to be using at the moment. Serious problems arise, however, when O'Flaherty has to write English dialogue for Gaelic-speaking Aran Islands peasants. The reader will search in vain for the cadences which Synge put into the mouths of the same peasants. But Corkery, O'Connor, and O'Faolain are literate in Gaelic too; why do they not suffer the same handicap as O'Flaherty? The answer is that for all practical purposes these three *are* illiterate in Gaelic, in the sense that, not being native speakers, they would never dream of attempting creative work in that language. For them it is a tongue which one speaks and listens to, doesn't perhaps read very much, and almost never writes. Thus it can serve as a touchstone for the language which one writes constantly and speaks so habitually that one can no longer hear what one is saying.

Another problem which faces the native speaker of Gaelic when he writes prose fiction in his mother tongue is the absence of literary as opposed to oral native models. Gaelic society died or fossilized before emerging from the feudal stage, so that there never was a middle class to demand or supply the realistic novel. Sustained narrative prose of any kind in Gaelic was until recently a desperate venture: a celebrated eighteenth-century attempt at autobiography can only be described as allegorical romance, while a political satire of the same period almost inevitably took the form of a burlesque hero-tale.[13] These are not clever devices, as they would be in English writers of the same period; the Gaelic writers simply *cannot* present their own experience more directly because they know no precedent for doing so. As the late Professor Gerard Murphy has written: "Though our knowledge of ancient Irish story-telling comes mainly from manuscript versions of the tales, there can be little doubt that Irish narrative tradition has on the whole been essentially oral."[14] Among the arguments offered by Murphy in support of his view, two strike me as particularly convincing; one is Professor Delargy's remark that

> No medieval Irish audience with its keen appreciation of a good tale, as marked in the eighth century as at the present day, would have listened very long to the story-teller if he were to recite tales in the form in which they have come down to us. Some of these manuscript tellings would occupy a reader or reciter not more than fifteen to twenty minutes.[15]

The other argument, Murphy's own, points to the fact that "several of the best manuscript texts begin well, but tail off badly as the story proceeds," and suggests that this

> . . . can be easily explained on the hypothesis of recording from oral recitation. Everyone who has tried to record Irish folktales from peasant reciters before the introduction of recording

machines has noticed the curtailment and imperfection which
tend gradually to creep into the recorded narrative owing to the
growing weariness of the reciter.[16]

Some of the shorter "tales," running to no more than a few
hundred words, must surely have been mere mnemonics in their
original form, skeletons on which the narrator would put flesh,
resembling the notes jotted on file card or shirt cuff for an hour-
long speech. To my mind the most convincing argument for the
oral origin of the manuscript tales is their anonymity. Typically,
every manuscript tale is anonymous, whereas every manuscript
poem of more than four lines has a poet's name prefixed—often
the wrong one.

Confronted with such a tradition, the Gaelic speaker who wants
to write modern fiction should look as far away from home as
possible and especially to countries whose oral tradition has long
gone into decline. Thus Ireland's leading Gaelic fiction writer of
this century (at least up to the date of his death in 1928), Pádraic
ÓConaire, read and recommended as models such writers as Chek-
hov, Conrad, and Anatole France.[17] Conversely, writers—and
especially short-story writers and dramatists—in languages whose
oral tradition has atrophied should turn for refreshment to languages which possess a living oral tradition. Irish writers of English
can do this without leaving their own country; indeed, as we have
seen, they still need not learn Gaelic if they go to the right part
of the country.

The two Irish fiction writers who have been most openly and
articulately concerned with the question of how to restore the oral
quality to fiction and especially to the short story are Frank
O'Connor and George Moore. The latter's claim to have been the
decisive influence on Synge, put forward in the preface to the Carra
Edition of *The Untilled Field*, seems so impudently mendacious that
one is inclined to disbelieve the rest of the preface also; but a
great deal of it happens to be true. Moore *did* start to write this
series of Irish short stories so that "Ireland's future writers should
have models"; many of the stories *were* translated into Gaelic and
made their first appearance in book form in that language; better
still, three of them *did* appear "in a Jesuit magazine," *The New
Ireland Review*, during 1902. These were translated into Gaelic
by the noted scholar Tadhg Ua Donnchadha. Moore clains that he
wrote three stories—"The Wedding Gown," "Alms-Giving," and
"The Clerk's Quest"—as well as a fourth, "So On He Fares," done
at the same time,

. . . in English rather than in Anglo-Irish, for of what help would
that pretty idiom, in which we catch the last accents of the original language, be to Tiagh Donoghue, my translater? As soon as
his translations were finished, my manuscripts were to be burnt;
but these first stories begot a desire to paint the portrait of my
country. . . .[18]

Needless to say, no manuscripts were burnt, and, once Moore had
decided that he would publish the English originals as well as the
Gaelic translations, he began to write the next stories in Anglo-
Irish, as he preferred to call it. The first of these new stories,
"The Exile," now opens *The Untilled Field*. Although rendered
from an omniscient viewpoint rather than from that of a specific
narrator, the narrative passages in this story are writen in Irish
English. (At this point I must abandon the term "the brogue," for
it implies self-conscious phonetic spelling, a feature which Moore
almost entirely eliminates; I shall discuss "Irish English" from
now on.)

Moore had spoken to Edward Martyn of providing "models"
not "*a* model" for the Irish writers of the future, and he proved
as good as his word. Among his stories are a wide variety of narrative approaches or, as we now tend to call them, points of view.
Beside omniscient narration in both Irish English and standard
English, we find a brilliant example of selective omniscience in
"Home Sickness," where the whole story is told in the third person
from a single viewpoint, that of James Bryden, the protagonist, in
the manner of Joyce's *A Portrait of the Artist*. Moore also adopts
more old-fashioned tricks to obtain a viewpoint which permits oral
narration: the group telling stories about the fire or the hackney-
car driver telling stories of the neighborhood to a visitor. In
"Julia Cahill's Cures," Moore adopts the latter convention, an out-
worn standby (I dare not call it hackneyed) of the upper-class
Irish writer and the English tourist, and extracts unusual irony
from it. The driver or "jarvey" believes implicitly that Julia's
curse has depopulated the townland, but the reader suspects that
the puritanism of the priest who drove Julia away has made the
people eager to emigrate. By one device or another, Moore keeps
his storytelling in or near the speaking voice; even in the Flau-
bertian "Home Sickness" we can almost hear James Bryden talking to himself as Moore probes his consciousness.

By the time Moore returned to the Irish short story in *A Story-
Teller's Holiday* (1918), he had become obsessed by the oral tradition, or at any rate by what he imagined it to be. Most of the book

consists of a storytelling contest between Moore and an imaginary County Mayo shanachie or oral storyteller with the quite un-Gaelic name of Alec Trusselby. The book is so entertaining that I must ask forgiveness for pointing out the harsh fact that most, perhaps all, of Alec's Irish stories do not belong to the modern folk tradition; they belong instead to the manuscript tradition, and furthermore, Alec could not have read them in manuscript without first taking a course in Middle Irish from, for example, Moore's friend Professor Kuno Meyer, who edited and translated at least one of them.[19]   Moore obviously knew little and cared less about adhering to the true Gaelic oral tradition but had grown more and more fascinated with the general problems of oral storytelling and of how to capture its apparent spontaneity on the printed page.   He had of course learned much about how to write spoken English from his autobiographies, and notably from *Hail and Farewell*, his highly personal account of the Irish Literary Revival, which was written between *The Untilled Field* and *A Story-Teller's Holiday*.

At one particular stage of his development as a writer of short stories, Frank O'Connor became acutely conscious of oral story-telling; in his own words:

> . . . I found that I had some talent as a broadcaster of stories, and was horrified to discover how the written word had robbed the story of its narrative impulse.   For some years I concentrated upon putting back the narrative impulse, and again and again radio producers had to be warned that when I was on the air I would drop whole passages or depart altogether from the script because those carefully arranged scenes and balanced sentences failed to get me beyond the microphone to listeners at the other side.   Generations of skilful stylists from Chekhov to Katherine Mansfield and James Joyce had so fashioned the short story that it no longer rang with the tone of a man's voice, speaking.[20]

"The tone of a man's voice, speaking"—those words sum up a great deal of what I have been trying to say about the IRISH short story.   It happens that O'Connor has been endowed by Providence with a phenomenal speaking voice: in resonance, range of pitch and breath control, it is one of the best untrained voices—if, in fact, it *is* untrained—that I have ever heard, O'Connor's record of "The Drunkard" and "My Oedipus Complex" might give the reader's thinking about the short story a whole new dimension.

But O'Connor means more than just the speaking voice when he uses the phrase "narrative impulse"; in a review of O'Flaherty written at about the same time as the above quotation, he reminds us that a short story must be "news" and he specifically invokes the oral tradition:

> "By the hokies, there was a man in this place one time by the name of Ned Sullivan, and he had a queer thing happen him late one night and he coming up the Valley Road from Durlas."
>
> .That is how a folk story begins, or should begin, and woe betide the storyteller whoever he may be who forgets that his story is first and foremost "news," that there is a listener he must grip by the lapel and shout at if necessary till he has attracted his attention.[21]

O'Connor goes on to admit that no printed short story should begin in this way, but he suggests that

> Joyce, like many other literary storytellers, is sometimes in danger of forgetting that his story is supposed to be "news" even if there is . . . no storyteller, properly speaking, and no audience.[22]

It is this awareness of a listener, of an audience, that almost all Irish storytellers except Joyce have in common; and if Joyce lacked it in *Dubliners* on the whole, he made up for this deficiency later—above all in *Finnegans Wake*. O'Connor was in danger of losing this awareness until he faced the invisible radio audience. But if he had been an oral storyteller, he could never have forgotten his audience, for it would have been seated right under his nose. This relationship between storyteller and audience is the indispensable component of the oral tradition; without it, the finest of storytellers loses his function and the largest and most varied of repertoires is forgotten. Professor Delargy has a touching anecdote about a storyteller named Seán Ó Conaill who found fewer and fewer opportunities for telling his stories as Gaelic and the old social life that went with it disappeared from his neighborhood:

> So, lest·he should lose command over the tales he loved, he used to repeat them aloud when he thought no one was near, using the gesticulations and the emphasis, and all the other tricks of narration, as if he were once again the centre of a fireside storytelling. His son, Pats, told me that he had seen his father thus engaged, telling his tales to an unresponsive stone wall, while herding the grazing cattle. On returning from market, as he walked slowly up the hills behind his old grey mare, he could be heard declaiming his tales to the back of the cart! In this way he kept a firm grip on stories which he had not told to an audience for over twenty years. . . .[23]

Few tradition-bearers can ever have possessed a fortitude equal to Seán Ó Conaill's. Most of them, like actors in our culture, must have audiences if they are to preserve and increase their skill.

And now, at last, let us look directly at this Irish oral tradition of which I have spoken so much, in order to see more clearly what elements it has and has not contributed to the Irish short story and to glean, if we can, some further insight into the poetics of the short story. With the help of Professor Delargy's epoch-making lecture to the British Academy, *The Gaelic Story-Teller*, we shall look first at the social setting, then at the traditional repertory, and finally at the storyteller himself.

The following quotation describes a *céilidhe* "in the little community of Gaelic-speaking fishermen in Teilionn, south-west Donegal":

> In every townland in the district there was at least one house to which, as a rule, the same literary clientele would resort during the nights of winter, usually from mid-September to 17 March; but the story-telling did not really start until *Oidhche Shamhna* [Hallowe'en] . . . . the old story-tellers seemed to be loath to tell folk-tales in their own homes, and would rather go to a *toigh áirneáil* [house of night-watching] than tell their tales in the presence of their own families. In the congenial atmosphere of the house of story-telling, undisturbed by the noise and prattle of children, their sensitive artistry was appreciated by the grown-up audience, mainly men, for whom these tales were intended. In return for the hospitality of the occupiers the guests attended to their simple wants, bringing turf from the stack, water from the well, and helping in various ways to put the house in order. The stage was soon set for the story-teller, a blazing turf fire provided the light, a stool or chair of the household's slender store was assigned to him in the place of honour beside the fire; and here he awaited the arrival of the visitors. . . . When the house was full to the door, the man of the house would fill his pipe with tobacco, and give it to the most respected guest. The person thus favoured smoked it for a while, then handed it back to its owner; after that it went round the company from one to another. By the time the last man had had his smoke, all the current topics of interest had been discussed, and the story-telling could now begin.[24]

Storytelling was not the only entertainment, for Gaelic songs were sung as well, but a sharp distinction was always preserved between the shorter and longer tales, which were usually not told by the same people. Indeed, the two kinds of storytellers bear different names in Gaelic:

> The Gaelic story-teller, properly so-called, is known usually as *sgéalai* . . . . *Seanchai* . . . . is applied as a rule to a person, man or woman, who makes a specialty of local tales, family-sages, or genealogies, social-historical tradition, and the like, and can recount many tales of a short realistic type about fairies, ghosts, and other supernatural beings. This type of narrative, now

often called *eachtra* or *seanchas,* approximates to the German *sage.* . . . These tales are still to be found in their thousands all over the country. But the number of persons—usually men—who can tell the *sean-sgéal* (*märchen*) is gradually being reduced; and soon but few will remain to recount in traditional style this once popular type of folk-tale.[25]

Elsewhere in his lecture Professor Delargy analyzes in considerable detail the differences of style, structure and content which distinguish the *sean-sgéal* from its shorter rivals. Aside from its sheer length and intricacy—one has been recorded that runs to 34,000 words—the former habitually contains a stylistic feature which is "almost exclusively confined to hero-tales or to *märchen* which have been fitted into the traditional pattern of oral heroic narrative": namely, the presence at intervals of

the traditional and often semi-obscure 'runs' without which . . . no hero-tale was complete. . . . The main function of the most elaborate of these embellishments is to impress the listener, and the more corrupt and unintelligible they are the greater the effect; but they serve also as resting-places for the story-teller in the recital of long, intricate tales, from which he can view swiftly the ground he has to cover. They are recited at a greater speed than the narrative proper.[26]

We need not wonder that the archaic *sean-sgéal* has had little or no influence upon Anglo-Irish literature, and especially upon the Irish short story. On the other hand, the short, realistic tale, as Professor Delargy points out, "is easily remembered, and can pass readily across cultural and linguistic frontiers. . . ."

To illustrate the point, let us look at the first part of J. M. Synge's *The Aran Islands.* There he has recorded two very different stories told him in English by the old storyteller Pat Dirane. The first tells of the Lady O'Conor; as Synge points out, it combines the plot of *Cymbeline* with that of the *Merchant of Venice,* although his recording of it, probably little more than a summary, runs to only a few thousand words; told as a *sean-sgéal* in Gaelic it might well run to five or ten times the length. A little later old Pat tells Synge an anecdote which would undoubtedly be classified as an *eachtra* or *seanchas.* In this a husband pretends to be dead, whereupon his wife immediately makes plans to marry a young neighbor. Pat Dirane told this folktale—which I take to be a variant of Aarne-Thompson Type 1350—with great realism, for he pretended to have participated in its events himself during a journey from Galway to Dublin.[27]   Such a tale, like all the Aarne-Thompson numbers from 1200 through 1999, could easily form the basis of an Irish—or for that matter a

Yiddish—short story. In fact, Synge based his one-act play *In the Shadow of the Glen* upon it. On the other hand, it seems unlikely that any playwright much later than Shakespeare could base a play upon the *märchen*—Aarne and Thompson actually classify it as a novella—about the Lady O'Conor.

Finally, let us take a look at the storyteller in action. Here is one striking description, the more impressive because it presents the storyteller not in the animated, crowded atmosphere of the *céilidhe* but before a chilly audience of one collector:

> His piercing eyes are on my face, his limbs are trembling, as, immersed in his story, and forgetful of all else, he puts his very soul into the telling. Obviously much affected by his narrative, he uses a great deal of gesticulation, and by the movement of his body, hands, and head, tries to convey hate and anger, fear and humour, like an actor in a play. He raises his voice at certain passages, at other times it becomes almost a whisper. He speaks fairly fast, but his enunciation is at all times clear. . . . He does not like to tell his tales on the Ediphone recording machine, as it hampers the movements he considers essential to heighten the effect of the story.[28]

You have noticed, of course, the contradiction explicit in this passage: first it is suggested that the gesticulation expresses the effect of the story upon the narrator; afterward the storyteller himself puts forward what I believe is the true view, namely that the gestures are an essential part of his communication with his audience. The gestures of a skilled Shakespearean actor do not express his own reaction to the poet's words; they are designed to enhance and make more specific the impact of those words upon the audience.

To reinforce this view, I should like to draw upon a personal experience. In May of 1956 I had the good fortune to attend one of six evenings of traditional singing, dancing, and storytelling staged in Dublin by an organization called Gael-Linn. The atmosphere of a *céilidhe* was reproduced as faithfully as possible in a stage set representing a kitchen in Connemara. I wrote while the experience was still fresh in my memory:

> The musicians and storytellers sat around on-stage, drinking and chatting whenever one of their number was not performing. All behaved with that odd combination of natural ease and keen sensitivity to their audience which stamps the best Abbey [Theatre actors].
>
> I have just enough Connacht Irish to recognize that Bartley Connelly's stories, with their strong prose rhythms and traditional alliterative "runs", were a banquet for the ear. But it was Dermot Cotter from Co. Cork who proved to be, in the

familiar Irish phrase, "as good as a play." I could hardly follow a word of his Munster Irish, but I did not need to. It was enough just to observe the currents of emotion playing over his young-old, crinkled face; to watch his uplifted blue eyes, suddenly lowered to meet the audience's at crises in the story; to follow the sparing gestures of hand or foot with which he dramatized certain passages. Here was a sort of Louis Jouvet of the folktale, an actor and an artist to his very fingertips.[29]

Not having been a Gaelic enthusiast in my youth, I had never attended a *céilidhe* proper, and thus this evening in Dublin revealed to me with startling clarity the explanation for two rather contradictory phenomena. On the one hand, I knew that Gaelic civilization had never developed a drama, mainly because it had never possessed any cities in which a permanent theater could have evolved, but I could not understand why the old Gaels had never felt the want of any such thing; now I realized that they had developed a completely satisfying equivalent in storytelling. On the other hand, I knew that a gift for acting was widely dispersed throughout the Irish countryside, although only a few cities and towns had a tradition of English-speaking theater; this fact too was now fully accounted for.

We now become certain of something that we had already suspected: when Frank O'Connor wrote of restoring the narrative impulse to the short story in the passage already quoted, he would have been wiser to write of the *dramatic* impulse, for that in fact was nearer to what he meant, as the content of radio performance already suggested. Current theorizing has adhered rigidly to an implied or explicit analogy between lyric poetry and the short story: feeling has been emphasized at the expense of action, symbol at the expense of plot. In pursuing this analogy, the theorists seem to have overlooked the converse trend in criticism of the lyric which tries to treat every lyric poem as implicit drama. I am thinking especially of what Reuben Arthur Grower has to say on the subject in his book *The Fields of Light,* where he develops the concept that "a poem is a dramatic fiction no less than a play."

In a recent article entitled "Problems of Collecting Oral Literature," Professor MacEdward Leach has written,

> As a result of our carrying over attitudes and techniques based on written literature we have failed to realize that folktale and much folksong are dramatic and that it is not the imagination of the audience that is appealed to but its sense of reality.[30]

Very true, but to my mind this statement need not imply that we should keep written literature and oral literature in watertight compartments. On the contrary, we should try to keep the lines of traffic open in both directions, so that attitudes and techniques based on oral literature can revivify written literature in periods of sterility. In practice, that is what happened at the beginning of the Romantic Movement in England and doubtless in Germany and France too. The dramatic quality of the popular ballad was incorporated into the Romantic lyric by Wordsworth and Coleridge, partly thanks to the influence of Burns. Not all the results were equally happy, but the lyric was unquestionably rescued from a morass of subjectivity into which it has never completely fallen back since. It is a moot point whether the influence of the folktale revivified Romantic short fiction or demoralized it, but I think a line could be traced from the Brothers Grimm via E. T. A. Hoffmann to Poe and the modern short story. At any rate, I hope I have shown that the Irish short story has constantly revitalized itself through renewed contact with the oral tradition; it may yet help the international short story to redeem itself from subjectivity by finding its way back to drama and the speaking voice.

Notes

1 Mary Lavin, *Selected Stories* (New York: Macmillan, 1959), p. vii.

2 See, for example, G. C. Duggan, *The Stage Irishman* (Dublin: Talbot Press, 1937) and J. O. Bartley, *Teague, Shenkin and Sawney* (Cork: Cork University Press, 1954).

3 New York: Columbia University Press, 1959.

4 William Carleton, *Traits and Stories of the Irish Peasantry,* 2 vols. (10th ed.; London: William Tegg, 1869), I, viii.

5 *Ibid.,* I, ix.

6 *Irish Penny Journal,* I (1840-41), 378.

7 Stith Thompson, *The Folktale* (New York: Dryden Press, 1946), p. 41. For "Index of Tale Types," see pp. 481-87.

8 Patrick Kennedy, *Legendary Fictions of the Irish Celts* (London: Macmillan, 1866), pp. 158-63.

9 James H. Delargy, *The Gaelic Story-Teller,* reprinted from the Proceedings of the British Academy, XXXI (London, 1945), pp. 6-7.

10 Frank O'Connor, *An Only Child* (New York: Knopf, 1961), pp. 250-51.

11 *New York Times Book Review,* June 10, 1956, p. 20.

12 *The Assassin* (London: Jonathan Cape, 1928), chap. 18. "The Landing," *The Stories of Liam O'Flaherty* (New York: Devin-Adair, 1956), pp. 31-39.

13 The autobiography is *Stair Éamuinn Uí Chléirigh (The History of Edmund O'Clery)* by Seán Ó Neachtain: see Robin Flower, *Catalogue of Irish Manuscripts in the British Museum,* II (London, 1926), 370-72; also *Gaelic Journal,* III, 35-36. The political satire is *Eachtra Thaidhg Dhuibh Uí Chróinin (The Adventures of Black Tadhg O'Cronin)* by Aodhagán Ó Rathaille, summarized in Vivian Mercier, *The Irish Comic Tradition* (New York: Oxford, 1962), pp. 166-69.

14 Gerard Murphy, *Saga and Myth in Ancient Ireland* (Dublin, 1955), pp. 4-5.

15 Delargy, *Gaelic Story-teller,* p. 32.

16 Murphy, *Saga and Myth* p. 7.

17 A. Ní Chnáimhín, *Pádraic Ó Conaire* (Dublin, 1947), p. 47.

18 George Moore, *The Untilled Field and The Lake* (New York, 1923), p. ix.

19 I mean Alec's story of Liadin *(sic)* and Curithir, first edited and translated by Meyer in 1902 as *Liadain and Curithir;* he republished part of the translation in *Selections from Ancient Irish Poetry* (London, 1911). Some Gaelic scholar should undertake a thorough study of Moore's sources for *A Story-Teller's Holiday.*

20 Frank O'Connor, *Stories* (New York: Vintage Books, 1956), p. vii. Paperback edition only.

21 *New York Times Book Review,* June 10, 1956, p. 1.

22 *Ibid.* For a fuller exposition of O'Connor's views on O'Flaherty, Joyce and the short story in general, see his *The Lonely Voice* (Cleveland & New York: World Publishing Co., 1963).

23 Delargy, *Gaelic Story-teller,* p. 12.

24 *Ibid.,* p. 19.

25 *Ibid.,* p. 6.

26 *Ibid.,* pp. 34-35.

27 John M. Synge, *Complete Works* (New York: Random House, 1935), pp. 326-33, 340-42.

28 Delargy, *Gaelic Story-teller,* p. 16.

29 Vivian Mercier, "The Dublin Tradition," *New Republic,* August 6, 1956, p. 22.

30 *PMLA,* LXXVII (1962), 335.

Comment

Richard J. Loftus

The short story came into its own rather late in the course of modern Irish literature. The poets of the literary revival were the first to win wide recognition—W. B. Yeats for his "Oisin," for example, and Douglas Hyde for his *Songs of Connacht*. Then, with the founding of the Irish National Theatre Society and the Abbey Theatre, the dramatist became the focus of attention. For many years these two genres dominated the literary movement. But in more recent times, in the past two decades especially, Irish writers have turned more and more to prose fiction and to the short story form in particular. That their achievement has been considerable is attested to by the remarkable success of such short story writers as Sean O'Faolain, Frank O'Connor, and Mary Lavin.

Like Irish poetry and drama before it, the Irish short story is invariably admired for its freshness and originality, for its direct and simple treatment of basic human situations. But, as Vivian Mercier makes clear, such admiration is largely mistaken. The unique character of the Irish short story has little to do with invention or originality. The qualities of simplicity and directness so often discerned are in fact largely derived from conscious imitation of a long literary and cultural tradition—a tradition that is unfamiliar to most sophisticated English and American readers. In another work Mercier has commented equally well on the pervasive influence of that tradition upon modern Irish writers:

> Whereas the writers of other Western countries have lately striven to re-establish contact with primitive modes of thought and feeling through the study of mythology, anthropology, and psychoanalysis, the Anglo-Irish writer has the past always at his elbow—in cold storage, so to speak—preserved in the Gaelic language and literature, in bilingual folklore, in Gaelic modes of thought and feeling and speech which have become part of the rural Anglo-Irish dialects.

HISTORY

The Ireland of 1838-41 was not yet the Ireland of the Great Famine which looms so large in our view of Irish experience. Yet Ireland's history already added up to a litany of misfortunes, quarrels, confiscations and conflicts variously traced to racial and religious enmity, a defective system of landholding and an equally bad social structure, widespread lack of education among peasants and laborers, and a rapid rise in births coupled with enormous poverty. An Anglo-Irish Protestant minority, including the well-to-do farmers, landlords, officials and clergy of the Anglican Church of Ireland, had long been in control. The majority of Irish laborers and peasants remained Catholic, but the rate of conversion to Protestantism, estimated by Kenneth Scott Latourette in his History of Christianity to have been "several thousand" during the first half of the 19th century had sufficiently alarmed leaders of the Roman Catholic Church into convening a national synod in 1850 to cope with the problem of proselytism.

John Appel

The Quarrel among the Roman Catholic Hierarchy over the National System of Education in Ireland, 1838-41*

Emmet Larkin

I

The quarrel that broke out among the Roman Catholic bishops in Ireland in early 1813 over the National System of Education was both unique and historic. Unique because, unlike most episcopal quarrels, it was furiously and bitterly fought out in the public press, and historic because it initiated one of the most intense phases in that long war between the Irish Church and the British State, which had been going on since the Reformation. The roots of this quarrel among the bishops in 1838 actually go back some twenty years, when the various English Protestant missionary societies launched their "New Reformation" in Ireland.

These evangelists founded schools, printed the Bible in Irish, distributed countless tracts and preached their word wherever they could find an audience. The Irish clergy had great difficulty in meeting the challenge, especially since the "Biblicals" were as well endowed with money as they were with fervor. The most serious threat of all, however, came from the schools founded by the Kildare Street Society in the early 1820's. The Catholics maintained that these schools were a mere mask for the proselytizing the children of their poor. Since the resources of the Irish Church were slender, it could not hope to meet the competition of the Society's schools which, in addition to large private donations, enjoyed a substantial annual subsidy from the government.

Therefore, when Lord Stanley proposed a resolution on Irish education in the House of Commons in 1831, which would abolish

---

The research for this article was made possible by grants-in-aid from the American Council of Learned Societies, the American Philosophical Society, the Social Science Research Council, and the Old Dominion Fund of the Massachusetts Institute of Technology.

121

the Kildare Street Society's quasi-legal and privileged financial position by setting up a system of national schools supported by the state, the Irish bishops, though hesitant about some of the terms, accepted the proposal as being at least less objectionable than the obnoxious Kildare Street system. The features of Stanley's proposal, which caused the Irish bishops the most concern, were that it was undenominational in principle, gave Catholics only two of the seven places on the governing national board, and allowed the bishops no final voice in either the texts published by the board or the appointment or dismissal of teachers and inspectors. The lead, however, was assumed by the Archbishop of Dublin, Daniel Murray, who accepted one of the Catholic places on the board, while the other was taken by his close friend and confidant, Anthony Blake, a prominent Dublin attorney. By 1838, some six years later, the government was expending £50,000 annually on some 150,000 children in 1,600 schools, 1,200 of which were managed by Catholics. Given the complexity and the implications of so vast a social experiment, the National System functioned efficiently and fairly, but not, it seemed, to the complete satisfaction of all the Irish bishops.

II

The first hint that there was anything to be regretted in the National System of Education was given at the annual meeting of the Irish bishops in Dublin in early February 1838 by William Higgins, the Bishop of Ardagh. Admitting there were differences of opinion on the principles and operations of the educational system, he wrote Paul Cullen, agent of the Irish bishops in Rome and rector of the Irish College there, that he "succeeded in putting the whole of the Bishops on the alert and produced such proofs as convinced all, that unless well watched, the Education as now carried on, was likely to undermine the authority of the Catholic Clergy, and ultimately introduce either positive errors or 'Indifferentism'."[1]

No one was more convinced that Bishop Higgins was correct in his assessment of the National System than that very strange and powerful personality, John MacHale, the Archbishop of Tuam. Soon after the meeting, Archbishop MacHale took the strange course of denouncing the National System in an open letter to Lord John Russell, then Home Secretary.[2] This was most unusual because, despite what Higgins had written to Cullen, the great majority of the bishops at the meeting had disagreed with the views expressed by Higgins, and MacHale was therefore appealing over their heads in the press to public opinion. Moreover, by his public denunciation of the system, he was implicitly criticising Archbishop Murray, who had been a member of the governing national board since its inception, and jeopardizing a fundamental guiding principle of the episcopal body—unity in action if not in national board since its inception, and jeopardizing a fundamental guiding principle of the episcopal body—unity in action if not in thought.

In his frontal assault on the National System, Archbishop Mac-Hale did not neglect to cover the vulnerable Roman flank. After the publication of his second open letter to Lord John Russell,[3] he forwarded both letters to Cullen in Rome with an explanation. "You may recollect," he wrote Cullen, "that when I was at Rome the New Education Board was formed after the Kildare Street Society and that even in its infancy it met with our disapprobation."[4] "It has since become more obnoxious," he continued, and, "Dr. Murray does not I think see the extent of its danger." "I felt it my duty lately," he explained, "to express my opinions on its dangerous tendency." What had been launched by Bishop Higgins as merely an alert in early February was now altered by Archbishop MacHale into an attack. He proceeded to mobilize the opinion of his clergy, and by the middle of April was able to report to Cullen that his three deaneries, amounting to more than 120 priests, "have expressed their unanimous concurrence in the Resolutions of all the Bishops of Ireland some years ago not to permit the Scriptures to be made a school book for children and not to relinquish the control which belongs to them over the selection of books and the choice of masters."[5]

The resolutions referred to by Archbishop MacHale had been passed in 1826, when the pressure from the Kildare Street Society's schools was becoming unbearable. It is indeed difficult to understand how he could have raised such a point at all, for the resolutions of 1826 had obviously been modified by the acceptance of the education proposal by the Irish bishops in 1831. Further, the archbishop, however reluctant, had not only been a party to the National System since its inception, but had remained a party to it for over six years without a word of protest. Moreover, he was still a party to it when he published his letters to Russell denouncing it, since the thirteen schools managed by the priests in his diocese were still in communion with the national board and accepting its grants. In fact, Archbishop MacHale did not finally break with the National System until some eighteen months after he first attacked it.

"It is my solemn belief," he now wrote Cullen, revealing what was really upsetting him, "that we have now more to fear for the purity of our faith than in former periods of more bitter persecution. The government is labouring to effect by fraud and wiles what past ones could not achieve by force and to supercede the authority of the local pastors and to place the entire education of the people in bodies over which they may exercise absolute control."[6] Obviously, Archbishop MacHale was still under the impression in 1838 that a state of war continued to exist between the Irish Church and the British State. The winning of Catholic emancipation nearly ten years before had changed nothing in his mind, except, perhaps, to give Catholics a bit more leverage and reduce the English to more subtle means of attack.

Soon after Archbishop MacHale published the second of his open letters, Archbishop Murray wrote his episcopal colleagues and inquired as to their opinions concerning the merits of the National System, on whose governing board he was, in effect, their representative. Their replies in March evidently gave such satisfaction that he did not think the issue serious enough to mention to Cullen until the end of April, and then, it seemed, only inadvertantly. "Dr. MacHale, you will have perceived," he remarked to Cullen, "is making a violent outcry, in opposition to the sentiments of the great majority of his Episcopal Brethren, against our National System of Education."[7] "But what is most surprising," he continued, "is that he bases his principle argument on an evident *misstatement*; namely that the Bible is under this system made a school book." "We were long struggling," Murray explained, "to obtain public aid, which could be safely applied towards the education of our poor and when obtained he seems desirous to wrest it from us, and throw it back into the hands of those who would employ it against us." "As for his pretended hope," concluded the archbishop, "of procuring a separate grant for the education of the Catholic poor, it is so utterly visionary that no rational person could entertain it for a moment."

After Archbishop MacHale's fifth open letter to Lord John Russell in early May, Archbishop Murray finally felt obliged to defend the National System at Rome, and submitted a "long history" of the system to Cardinal Fransoni, the prefect of propaganda. At the same time, he forwarded the rules of the system to Cullen to be put into an "Italian dress."[8] In what amounted to a postscript to his "long history" a few weeks later, Murray met another of MacHale's chief objections to the system by pointing out to Cullen for the benefit of propaganda "that the Commissioners do not appoint School Masters; but accept or approve of those who are proposed by the local managers throughout the Country; and as by far greater majority of the principal of these local managers are Priests it follows that no master can be appointed without their approbation."[9] "All that the Commissioners have to do with the Teachers," he continued, "is to see that they be competent persons—of moral character—and that they do not attempt any undue influence with regard to the religion of their Pupils."

When Cullen in reply requested copies of the school books and Scripture Extracts—another sore point with MacHale—for the inspection of propaganda, Murray forwarded them immediately remarking—"the Extracts being not intended for Controversy, but moral instruction, are translated directly from the Hebrew and Greek; but they differ in no point affecting faith or morals from the Vulgate."[10]

While Murray was thus busily defending the National System at Rome, Archbishop MacHale had successfully persuaded a large number of his brother bishops as to the dangers of the system. In what certainly was a remarkable tribute to his own powerful personality, MacHale had converted all of his suffragens, six in number, and could now muster a minority of ten in a hierarchy of twenty-six. One of his suffragens, the Bishop of Galway, George J. P. Browne, broke the news of his own change of heart, and that of his fellow suffragens, to Archbishop Murray early in August. He also informed him that he felt it his duty to make his views public. Murray was furious and he wrote Browne a very stiff reply indeed

> That Yr. Lp. should exclude from the flock entrusted to your spiritual care, any system which according to your judgment would be injurious to them is a duty which I would expect from Yr. Lp. But Yr. Lp. must be aware that very many of Your Broker Prelates, of sound judgment and undoubted zeal, conscientiously differ with Yr. Lp. on this point; and I now put it to the conscience of Yr. Lp. whether it wd not be somewhat rash, and of course not free from crime, to issue any public Document which would by implication, condemn them, while under a sense of duty as Strong as that which operates on the mind of Yr. Lp. They are anxious to spread among their Flocks this same National system the advantages of which they appreciate highly. Yr. Lp. expresses a belief that Yr. Brother Bishops of the Province share in your sentiments. This surprises me exceedingly. Their several letters written to me in March indicate no such feeling, and

I am inclined to hope that their change of opinion has not been
as sudden and unaccountable as that of Yr. Lp.[11]

Archbishop Murray then instructed his secretary, Canon Hamilton, to forward the letters written in March by the "Connaught
Bishops" to Rome, for if their "sentiments have undergone an unfavorable change, the reasons which produced it will then be
better understood."[12] Murray's very stiff letter to Browne had its
effect, for Hamilton also reported to Cullen that at a recently
held provincial meeting of the bishops of Connaught, with Archbishop MacHale at their head, "it was unanimously resolved not
to publish any document against the National System, without
having consulted all the Bishops of Ireland."[13] "From this wise
decision," Canon Hamilton concluded, "nothing I hope will induce
them to depart."

Though the bishops did not openly come to blows in the press
for several months more, their partisans conducted a furious
polemic. Finally, in late October 1838, Archbishop Murray, exas-
perated by the attacks, published a detailed reply to the objections
made against the National System, taking particular care to avoid
personalities by concerning himself with the issues.[14] A week
later, however, Archbishop MacHale took Murray to task in a
letter which was remarkable for its irrelevancy.[15] "From a feeling of respect for him," wrote MacHale of Murray, "we suffered
much to pass over in silence which would have called forth our
earlier animadversion and remonstrance." "It was only when we
saw," he explained, "the vicious system teemed with evils which
no zeal or piety on the part of any individual member of the
body, however active, could correct, that we raised our feeble voice
to protest against a scheme of education which threatened such
serious dangers to the fold."

In his rejoinder Archbishop Murray finally hammered Mac-
Hale with the mailed fist, never forgetting, however, to wear his
velvet glove. In questioning the "logic" of MacHale's argument
that the inspectors regulated the quantity of religious instruction
in the national schools, Murray asked—"Could your Grace have
been really serious in drawing from such premises such a conclusion?"[16] "Perhaps so," he wryly remarked, "for even old Homer
himself, while engaged in composing his undying works, was
sometimes, as we read, known to slumber; and if he were not
blind, I would add with his eyes open." Murray then went on to
point out that MacHale had only begun to complain about the
National System after an application of his for a grant for a
school in his diocese had been refused by the commissioners.

"What new light," commented Murray, "this disappointment may have thrown upon the National System, it is not for me to guess." "But," he pointed out, "it appears that, on the following February, in a meeting of the Bishops, from which a severe illness compelled me to be absent, and after some of the Prelates had retired, your Grace, as I am informed, thought proper, without any previous communication with me, to animadvert on the Commissioners, in no very measured terms, for their imputed partiality in the distribution of the education grant, and to harangue the meeting on the dangerous tendency of the system which they administered."

Archbishop MacHale, in his reply to Murray, once again refused to come to grips with the issues raised or the charges made by his opponent. He insisted on talking about what the system might become rather than what the system actually was. "From the extraordinary power," MacHale fearfully maintained, "now claimed by the state over a mixed education, it would soon claim a similar despotic control over mixed marriages, and strive to stretch its net over all ecclesiastical concerns."[17] "It would never want subservient instruments," he added most insultingly. This public exchange, which certainly exceeded the bounds of episcopal moderation, only served to increase the bitterness between the contending parties, and expose the carefully preserved fiction of episcopal unity.

Moreover, and more important, Rome was scandalized by the public quarrel among the Irish bishops. Murray wrote Cullen explaining that for eight months he had allowed himself and his brother bishops to be assailed in the press until finally people were beginning to believe that the oft-repeated charges were true. "Still," he concluded rather dryly, "if the H. See think it advisable to decide otherwise, or even to hint its disapprobation of any other part of my proceedings in this affair, I will at once retire from the Board, and leave the education grants entirely in the hands of Protestants as before, conscious that in union with the great body of my Brother Bishops I had done all in my power to avert the mischief to religion which will inevitably follow."[18] Cullen had also obviously dropped a necessary hint to Archbishop MacHale. "It was with great reluctance," MacHale replied, "I was first induced to expose the errors and dangers of the System on account of his Grace of Dublin's connection with it."[19] "Nothing," he explained, "but the exposure of the system at large and in detail could shake the treacherous Confidence of many of the Catholics or intimidate our enemies from following up their inroads on our faith and discipline." "Do not you [be upset]" he counseled Cullen in conclusion, "if any in Rome be scandalized by our *Episcopal quarrel.* That part is, I trust, over and will do no harm."

Meanwhile, Cullen had informed Archbishop Murray that the Roman theologians would most likely condemn the scripture extracts. Such a decision, the archbishop pointed out in his reply, would only make Catholics a laughing stock, and give credence to Protestant claims that they dare not let their deluded followers read the Bible since it would only expose the impostures of the Church of Rome. His only desire, Murray continued, was to raise the poor "out of their degrading inferiority."[20]

When Bishop Higgins received the news of the expected condemnation, he was elated. "I feel tempted to be very vain," he wrote Cullen. "The points to which you think Rome will object, are precisely those, which in our local meeting, I brought before the assembled Prelates."[21] "From the very beginning," he continued, "I felt the Episcopal Authority was usurped by laymen and heretics—the distinctive dogmas of our Holy Religion carefully omitted in the school books; and that under the name of Christian forbearance between Catholic and Prostestant latitudenarianism was treacherously sought to be instilled into the minds of the children." In a grudging fashion, Higgins was willing to admit that the provision of schools for Catholic children might, at first, cause some inconvenience, "but, even so, why endanger the faith or morals of our poor people." The propaganda, as usual, however, confounded all expectations by referring the objections of its theologians to Archbishop Murray, and thus virtually reopened the whole question.

III

Since Rome had so adroitly sidestepped the whole issue of an appeal, the supreme question now was what would the Irish bishops do at their annual general meeting to be held on January 22, 1839 in Dublin? As usual, the Bishop of Ardagh was first to contact Cullen with a remarkably indiscreet letter marked "PRIVATE." "It is now 5 o'clock P.M.," Higgins wrote, not losing a minute, "and we have just terminated our second day's stormy debate on the subject of the present system of National Education." The Bishop of Limerick, seconded by the Bishop of Kilmore, Higgins reported, had proposed a resolution stating "that the present system was without a blemish," while he had seconded Archbishop MacHale's amendment—"that as a serious difference of opinion existed among the Bishops on the important matter, it should be referred to the Holy Father for his decision." "I say with much affliction," lamented Higgins to Cullen, "that nothing could surpass the *secular views* and want of candour on the part of our opponents." "Could you ever imagine that an Irish Bishop," he continued, mortified, "would stubbornly and not very respectfully refuse to consult the successor of Peter in his doubts and difficulties—yet sixteen have acted in this manner!!!"

> I write however this evening that you may not *lose a moment* in putting the Cardinal Prefect or His Holiness [in] possession of all the details, that they may stand on the alert, and give no opinion before they receive our statement, which shall be forwarded as soon as we can. If the others write, their communications should be received with caution, particularly any books or Regulations, of the Board of the Commissioners as, heretic like, *they change,* or modify these things *ad captandum*: of this we have proofs. It is needless to request you will keep this a profound secret. I have no objection however that you would communicate it to the Pope or Cardinal; but afterwards burn the letter. I shall soon write again . . . . P. S. . . . . Everything friendly from his Grace of Tuam. He would write if he had not known that I do.[22]

Perhaps Cullen did not burn this interesting letter because he was impressed by a previous comment of Higgins in reference to someone else in another letter. "He enjoins strict secrecy," wrote Higgins, "forgetting that every real contract must have *two* consenting parties."[23]

A week later Higgins forwarded the promised petition signed by the ten bishops who supported the minority view, in which they outlined their objections to the National System.[24] He followed this up the next day with additional objections of his own, which give an excellent insight into the apprehensive mentality of the minority. The books recommended by the board, Higgins maintained, were full of "Indifferentism or Arianism."[25] As proof, he offered a book by the Protestant Archbishop of Dublin, William Whately, and also a member of the National Board of Education, entitled, *Lessons on the Truth of Christianity.* "This production," Higgins argued, "calls everything into doubt—talks of nothing but 'Christianity' in the vague or rather Arian sense of the word, incessantly insinuates the Redeemer to be nothing more than the adopted son of God." "Whatever may result from our application," he concluded lyrically, "we have the consolation to feel, that we have not been 'dumb dogs' and that we have with us the Catholic feeling of Ireland, and the honor of counting among our opponents, all the bad priests, lukewarm and Castle-hack Catholics, as well as the heretical or Voltarian Liberals of the Empire.[26] Some months later Cullen had occasion to mention Dr. Whately's production to Archbishop Murray. "With respect to the little book on the truth of Christianity which you mentioned," replied the archbishop tartly, "it is quite clear that you did not read it." "In the 3rd page," he continued, "the object for which it was written is truly stated to be, not what you were told, but 'to suggest such reasons to those who believe in Jesus Christ as may serve to protect them from the insidious artifices of Infidels, and enable them to strengthen the faith of others, or to restore those who may have fallen from Christian profession.' "

Some days after its conclusion, Archbishop Murray also referred to the proceedings at the annual meeting in a letter to Cullen. Sixteen bishops, including three of the four archbishops, he wrote, "stood firm in their decided approval of the National System of education, and considered it unnecessary to annoy the Holy See on a subject which they found by experience to be not only safe but advantageous to Religion."[28] "I have received from Propaganda," he added, "the objections made against the Scripture extracts; and as soon as I can get a moments leisure I will answer them. Some of them are exceedingly foolish." He also mentioned that the Primate, the Archbishop of Armagh, William Crotty, would forward the resolutions passed by the majority.

A week later Dr. Crotty described to Cullen, for the benefit of Propaganda, how he had asked all the prelates individually to state their views, and they "all candidly confessed they had not discovered in it anything contrary to Faith or morality."[29] Archbishop MacHale had specifically complained, Crotty reported, of a Catholic schoolmaster in his diocese who had become a Protestant, and the National Board refused to dismiss or punish "the apostate." To this Archbishop Murray had replied that the board had no power to dismiss or punish any man because of a change in his religious views, adding "that the exercise of such power, would in many cases be injurious to the Catholic interest, as the conversion of heretics to the Catholic faith is very common at the present time, in every part of the British Empire." When MacHale objected to the scripture extracts, he was told that he could exclude them from every school in his diocese if he was so minded. The majority then, according to Archbishop Crotty, offered to appoint a "Committee of Prelates" to examine all the books recommended by the board in order that there might be no doubt about their orthodoxy. MacHale "rejected this amicable proposal, and seemed unwilling to adopt any terms of concilation." "The Prelates then," concluded Crotty, "passed their resolutions—which are only an open acknowledgment of facts that cannot be denied."[30]

Though the annual meeting actually settled nothing, it did clarify the issues for everyone. There was no doubt that Archbishop MacHale was "determined to use every means in his power" to destroy the National System,[31] and those means included the authority of Rome. The specific complaints about books, lessons, teachers and inspectors made by the MacHale party were either isolated instances in a vast complex or fearful previsions of no substance. What was really at the heart of the matter for Archbishop MacHale and his colleagues had been voiced again in early February by Bishop Higgins. "In my conscience," he had writted Cullen, "I believe and this belief is shared by all the Prelates who signed our reference to Rome, that the English Government hope to accomplish by this System what fire and sword could not do—the extinction of the Catholic Faith in Ireland."[32]

But what real evidence was there for any threat to the faith? "For the last six years," wrote Michael Blake, Bishop of Dromore, to Cullen, "no instance of any child having been seduced from the Catholic Faith has been alleged even by those who are most hostile to the new system."[33] Blake summed up the issue when he pointed out to Cullen that those "who side with Dr. MacHale are for the most part influenced by apprehensions as to what might possibly happen hereafter."

Both sides now settled down, rather uneasily, to await the pleasure of Rome. In early March, Archbishop Murray finally found time to reply to the objections, or "Animadversions," made by propaganda's theologians to the scripture extracts. In asking Cullen to submit them to the Pope he remarked—"For altho' the opponents of the National System do not, as I am informed, scruple to reckon you on their side, your judgment will, I am sure, be an honest one; and that is all I could desire."[34]

Less than a month later, Cullen wrote Murray that it was more than likely the scripture extracts would be condemned by propaganda, not withstanding his defense of them. "Should the Holy See," warned Archbishop Murray in his reply, "be induced to adopt any hostile proceeding against them, there is but one course left for me to pursue; to reject what it rejects, and to retire from all future superintendence of Catholic interests in the National Board. Government may easily find some abler and more fortunate Person to supply my place."[35] "You think," wrote the archbishop, about a month later, to Cullen, who had obviously made the mistake of trying to console him, "I am too much troubled about the result of the Education question. The subject is of too much moment not to command anxiety about it."[36]

Meanwhile Archbishop MacHale was also disturbed about the news from Rome, but for a different reason. In early March, Cullen reported that two very prominent English Catholics, Lords Shrewsbury and Clifford, were in Rome, maintaining that Drs. MacHale and Higgins were subordinating the interests of religion to Irish politics. MacHale informed Cullen it was a plot, and the English government was at the bottom of it all.[37] Higgins was his usual indiscreet self. "If Rome forms its opinion of the Irish Church," he wrote Cullen, "from the calumnies or stupidity of Englishmen the fault is not ours."[38] Two weeks later, Higgins reported he was on his way to Rome with John Cantwell, the Bishop of Meath, and another strong opponent of the National System.[39] En route, Higgins wrote Cullen a note from Avignon marked *Very Private.* "We met Dr. McGettigan in London," he remarked, referring to the amiable Bishop of Raphoe, "and it is probable he will arrive in Rome before us."[40] "His Lordship," continued Higgins, "entertains very strange ideas about education . . . and would it not be well so to manage matters that he shall have no opportunity of delivering his sentiments on these subjects, or that of the calumny against Dr. MacHale, etc. before our arrival." "You know already," he concluded rather lamely, "that I look upon him to be a well-meaning prelate, and you will not I trust be disedified at the hints just thrown out."

Finally, in late June, propaganda condemned the scripture extracts, and Archbishop Murray immediately appealed the decision personally to the Pope. "You will be surprised to learn," Murray informed Cullen, "that our Gov't was in possession of the sentiments of Propaganda regarding the System of National Education for some days before your letter on that subject reached me."[41] The government was aware, he explained, "that Dr. Higgins was made the Bearer of the Verbal assurance to Doctor MacHale from Propaganda that the S. Cong disapproved the books used for Catholic instruction and would immediately direct me to retire from the Board." Lord Ebrington, the Lord Lieutenant, then sent for him, Archbishop Murray continued, and gave him a letter containing "an authoritative assurance that we can have no hope of public aid for education on terms more favorable than those on which the National System is conducted." "Lord Abrington," Murray explained, after asking Cullen to submit the letter to the Pope, "has assuredly underrated the disasterous consequences which would ensue from any attempt of the Authorities of Rome to put down the National System."[42] "In fact," it was Murray's candid opinion, "it is doubtful if even the Holy See itself could succeed against the clear convictions of the people." "And if it did," he added, reminding Rome that Pyrrhic victories are of little use, and especially to Irish Catholics, "the education grant would be thrown into the hands of Protestants, and we should be all back under all the evils inflicted by the Kildare Place System." Would the Pope, however, consent to hear Archbishop Murray's appeal against the decision of propaganda? After a month of anxious waiting, Murray was "rejoiced to find that the supreme Guardian of our Faith has Himself vouchsafed to look into the nature of our Education System."[43]

When the Pope finally decided to take action some months later, it was in the genuine Roman tradition. He simply reopened the whole question by asking each of the contending parties to send a priest as deputy to represent their cases. Archbishop Murray immediately dispatched two of his ablest priests, both of whom had been trained in Rome and knew Italian. Archbishop MacHale hesitated, however, and offered the thought that "one or two *Bishops*" from "*both sides*" should go rather than the requested "*ecclesiastic*."[44] Bishop Higgins was also of the opinion that to send a mere priest was "unwise" because the question was too important.[45]

A month later MacHale was still having difficulty finding a deputy to send to Rome. He thought that Higgins should go, or if it were really necessary he was prepared to make the sacrifice himself. "Now is their time," MacHale wrote referring to Rome, "to strike the salutary blow. The opportunity lost may never be effectually recovered."[46] In a long postscript to this letter, Higgins added he thought MacHale should go to Rome. "For God's sake," he exhorted Cullen, who was supposed to be neutral, "throw all your energies into the scale of justice— endeavor to *reclaim* the Dublin deputies, and save us from the cruel persecution of pretended friendship." In early December, MacHale had still not found a priest with the language, theology, and "hearty zeal" to send to Rome. He again offered to come himself, and was very pleased that Cullen had deferred his visit to Ireland at this critical moment.[47]

Indeed, the pressure on those opposed to the National System had been mounting steadily since August when the Pope had taken matters into his own hands. When Rome designated a priest rather than a bishop as deputy it was a strong hint that Rome would be embarrassed by either a visit from MacHale or the return of Higgins, who had received some very explicit assurances from the propaganda for Archbishop MacHale the previous June. When Cullen, in attempting to explain to Higgins how the tide had turned, mentioned that Rome must often look to the whole rather than the parts, the Bishop of Ardagh had some very blunt things to say about expediency and Rome. "I am really scandalised," he confessed to Cullen, "that the abominable Education Systems of Prussia, Austria, etc. should at all influence Rome in her decisions on Irish questions; and the more so, as *I know* that those systems are detested by the Cardinals."[48] "If our affairs here," he added at the height of his moral indignation, "must be judged of, and decided upon, by the rules of political expediency, I fear such a state of things will arise as we would all very much deplore."

Then Higgins went on to outline a scheme which made the alleged Roman expediency pale in its shade. If Rome and its cardinals

> . . . . are so mortally afraid of giving offense to open tyrants or perfidious heretics, can they not at least express themselves freely to each Bishop of Ireland, ordering them to follow the intimation thus privately conveyed, as though it were the result of his own maturer deliberations. In addition to this, they might (publicly) address us *as a body* through the Primate, expressing their unwillingness to interfere, and *strongly* exhorting us to terminate the controversy ourselves.[49]

The following week Higgins repeated his proposal, but suggested that the Pope should take the lead rather than the cardinals.[50] Though he had not consulted his brother bishops, Higgins was confident that those on his side would agree with his plan. What is there to be said about a proposal as fantastic as it was dishonest? Nothing, perhaps, except to note that a prolonged state of war produces some strange moral aberrations.

When it was rumored in Ireland in the middle of December, 1839 that the education question had been settled in favor of Dr. Murray and his supporters,[51] the pressure on the minority became so great that even Archbishop MacHale showed signs of cracking. Up to this point MacHale had always concentrated on the system rather than the motives of its supporters, which he always left in the hands of Bishop Higgins. MacHale confided to Cullen, shortly before Christmas, that "the impression in Ireland is that having failed by argument and fair means the deputies were employed in conveying as covertly as they could hints tantamount to menaces in case of an adverse decision."[52] Archbishop MacHale had also more or less respected the neutrality of Cullen's difficult position as agent of all the Irish bishops. Now, in asking Cullen to write as often as he could, MacHale assured him if he marked anything private he would have a corresponding confidence. There was also at this time a good deal of pressure on MacHale from his closest supporters. The archbishop had been injudicious enough in November to appear again in the public press on the education question. Rome viewed this as an act of gross disrespect, especially since the Pope had taken the matter in to his own hands. Cullen wrote Bishops Higgins and Cantwell to use their best efforts to keep MacHale out of print.[53]

Meanwhile there had recently appeared a series of articles by a Dublin priest in the *Evening Post*. It was Cantwell's opinion, expressed to Cullen, that the articles would "damage the Board and its Patrons more than all that has yet occurred."[54] Indeed, the priest, Thaddeus J. O'Malley, had maintained that if Catholic primary education on the Continent were any example, it would be better to have all such matters in the hands of the state rather than the Church. "Believe me," Higgins wrote Cullen, referring to Father O'Malley, "this man is the paid agent of Government for schismatical purposes, and unless silenced at once from writing on clerical concerns will do mischief."[55] Rome will have nothing to fear in Ireland, he concluded characteristically, "provided they do not hearken to bad Catholics, *weak* Bishops, or heretical lies and exaggerations." "It only shows," commented MacHale the same day, "if Priests are taught to look to the patronage of the World what a Spirit of Ecclesiastical insubordination we shall soon have in Ireland."[56] "And yet," he added, "it is such Catholics and such Priests the Board and its Masters would wish to have as the *liberal* lecturers of the training Schools. Downright professing heretics would do far less harm."

Given the delicate state of Irish affairs in Rome, however, the articles were a serious source of embarrassment to Dr. Murray. Besides being on the Dublin mission, Father O'Malley was already very well known, not to say notorious in Rome, and especially to the Pope, who before his elevation had been Prefect of Propaganda, and had a great deal to do with Father O'Malley, who had been involved in a celebrated schism in Philadelphia, where had sided with the lay trustees of his parish against his bishop and had been excommunicated for his conduct. "Mr. O'Malley," Archbishop Murray tried to explain to Cullen, "is not one of our Priests, and is therefore under less control than if he were. He came here uncensured after having made his peace with Rome, and got leave to say Mass; as it is hardly safe in a Country like this, to drive a Priest of some talent and strong feelings to extremities without a real necessity."[57]

While the Irish bishops were thinking only in terms of a papal decision, and the moves and countermoves likely to influence it, Rome had been quietly attempting to persuade them to come to an amiable arrangement among themselves, and thereby avoid the judgment of Solomon. Cullen had tried to initiate the policy early in September in a letter to Archbishop Murray, but he received only an unequivocal declaration of no compromise.[58]

Archbishop MacHale was even more explicit some two months later. "The present system," he wrote Cullen, ". . . is too radically vicious for reform. Delindas est Carthaga, or Rome and its faith and influence will have in the accursed system a rival that will soon change the minds and affections of the people of Ireland."[59] Rome, meanwhile, still continued to press for an arrangement. She hinted broadly, through Cullen, that the approaching annual meeting of the bishops in Dublin in February 1840 would be the moment to effect the accommodation. Two years of bitter quarreling, however, had taken a heavy toll on that store of good faith which is so necessary to any real agreement.[60]

IV

The annual meeting, which began on February 13, 1840, was variously reported by the contending parties. "We have been discussing," Archbishop MacHale was the first to inform Cullen on Feburary 14, "the terms on which an accommodation could be effected up to this moment."[61] In fact, MacHale had taken the initiative by proposing a resolution whose form spelled compromise, but whose spirit breathed war.

> That though we should prefer a system of an exclusively separate education yet we should provided it meet the approbation of his Holiness allow [the word "accept" is crossed out] a mixed System founded on the resolutions of the Archbishops and Bishops in the year 1826: that in order that the fulfillment of those resolutions may be secured we deem it but just on the part of the Government to give us the guarantee of an act of Parlia-

ment pledging that in the Board constituted to conduct this System there shall be as many Catholics as all the Protestants professing different creeds fairly representing the four Provinces and that of those Catholics there shall be two Bishops from each selected by their Co Provincials to watch over the integrity of faith and morals as well as the equitable disbursement of the funds in various districts.[62]

"The hopes of yesterday," MacHale wrote Cullen the next day, "are realized unanimously on conditions which will be laid before the Lord Lieutenant."[63] To say the least, Archbishop Mac-Hale was no fool. He realized better than anyone, given the political situation in the country, and especially in Parliament, the government could not agree to the proposed conditions. Yet, he also knew his episcopal brethren could not oppose the conditions without compromising themselves at Rome. In short, the tactic was to use the petition as a wedge to divide the bishops who supported the National System from the government.

In informing Cullen, a week later, that the petition to the Lord Lieutenant had been "unceremoniously rejected," MacHale's artfulness became apparent. He told Cullen, "We could not with propriety venture on any suggestion."[64] "There is no doubt," he added suggestively, "but the Pope can now with the good wishes of all the Prelates (for they are now committed) made a stand and insist on our arrangement as the basis of any accommodation." "There is still," he prompted Cullen, "an easier course than any. If Dr. Murray were paternally advised to retire from the Board the Prelates whose feeble and lingering support it receives an account of a deference to him would abandon it to its fate." In addition to counseling Murray to retire from the board, MacHale suggested that Rome should also warn all the prelates against the National System, and recommend that they all petition the government for separate grants for the schools in their dioceses. His suggestion that these petitions should express "a confidence that a government distinguished for its Magnanimity, Wisdom, and Justice will never refuse so just a boon to a loyal and faithful people," was only a further indication of his bad faith, for no one in Ireland believed less in either the government's good intentions or the people's loyalty to it than did Archbishop MacHale.

The postscript to this letter was, of course, written by Bishop Higgins. "The best use I can make of this space," he added frantically, "is to implore you to cause his Holiness, if you have it in your power to direct us all to petition for separate grants, cautioning us against the present System. For God's sake exert all your influence."

Archbishop Murray's account of the annual meeting to Cullen included a number of things MacHale had neglected to mention. Surprisingly enough, Murray reported that those opposed to the National System "gave up the claim for a separate grant for the education of Catholics as unattainable."[65] Yet, as has been noticed, a week after they are reported by Murray as admitting that separate grants are unattainable, Drs. MacHale and Higgins are urging Rome to instruct the Irish bishops to petition the government for them. If the government had rejected what was less objectionable, what was the point in urging a more objectionable course, except to drive even deeper the wedge between the government and the bishops who supported the National System, and to drive it with a Roman hammer for good measure?

By this time, however, Archbishop Murray was furious with the dissenting bishops. "The ten discontented Prelates," he informed Cullen, "declared open war in the public papers on the very day of our General Meeting."[66] Murray accused them of not only eating their cake but of wanting even more of it, while loudly declaring it was not fit for human comsumption. "And surely," he pointed out to Cullen, "at least nine of the Dissident Prelates cannot think the system so very dangerous to the faith of their people as their public denunciations would seem to indicate or they could not allow this heretical plant to shoot up and thrive under their eyes in every part of their respective Dioceses." "Well," he asked, after noting that only MacHale had disassociated the some thirteen schools in his diocese from the board, "how many schools have the other dissenting Prelates withdrawn from under the National System?" "Not one," he replied, "and no wonder: for according to the reports of the various Prelates, the children of Parishes where there are National Schools have been found much better instructed in the principles of their religion, than ever the children of those Parishes were before." "In the County of Wexford," Murray pointed out, referring to the diocese of Ferns, whose bishop opposed the system, "there are thirty three N. Schools. Of twenty nine of those Schools Priests are the principle Patrons, and the regular correspondents of the Board; and whatever aid the Board supplies passes thro' their hands." "The County of Longford," he continued, referring to Higgins, "is a skirt of the Diocese of Ardagh. In that County there are twenty two National Schools, of which twenty one are under Catholic Priests." "Yet," Murray noted, "the Prelates of Ferns and Ardagh are among the warmest opponents of the Board, the heretical tendency of which they have the other day denounced in the Public Papers." "The Bishop of Elphin," he cited another example, "was lately in treaty with a Catholic of Dublin for a spot of ground whereon to erect an additional National School in his Diocese, and entrusted the conclusion of it to the V.G. [Vicar General] Yet his Lp. is outwardly an opponent of the System." "But why go thro' them all," he concluded in exasperation. "The schools which are daily spreading in their Dioceses with their permission bear testimony against them if they think the system bad."

Several days later, Murray was still so wrought up that he wrote Cullen a long, angry postscript to this letter. "This apparent double-dealing of so many of our Prelates," he said, "who denounce in word what they encourage in practice, has exceedingly scandalised the intelligent portion of the Catholic Body; and lower'd in the minds of Protestants, to a most humiliating degree, the character of our Prelacy."[67] "To the Government," continued Murray, indicating that MacHale had not been without some success in driving his wedge, "their proceedings appear to be utterly factious, not having seemingly any real principle of Religion to rest upon: and I fear much that the mischievous effects of those proceedings will be felt beyond the boundaries of these Islands to the great disadvantage of our numerous fellow Catholics who are spread throughout the extensive colonies of Britain abroad." What was certain, Murray maintained, was that the government was watching the progress of the education question at Rome, and that the ministers seemed to be acquainted with every step that was taken there. "I hope however," he remarked pointedly to Cullen, "that all the information they receive is not accurate." "I lately saw a letter addressed to the Government by one of their Diplomatic Agents in Italy (a Protestant) which stated that nothing could be decided on the Education question until the arrival of Dr. MacHale's Deputy; but that in reality he did not need one, for that all thro' he had a most efficient one in the President of the Irish College." "I need not say," Murray concluded, even more pointedly, "how galling this intelligence would be to the great majority of the Irish Prelates if they could place the slightest reliance on a piece of information, which for many reasons, they could not possibly anticipate."

Several days later, MacHale began what can only be described as another journalistic donnybrook.[68] In a Lenten pastoral to his clergy and the faithful, MacHale claimed that the unanimity of the bishops in their petition to the Lord Lieutenant for a modification of the National System was proof positive that the system as it existed was inconsistent with the maintenance of the Catholic religion in Ireland.[69] Murray vigorously denied that the petition implied any such thing, and soon their partisans, clerical and lay, were once again freely swinging at each other in the rough and tumble of Irish journalism.[70]

Finally, when the Bishop of Kilmore wrote Cullen early in April that the public controversy was not only disrespectful to the Pope's sacred authority, but was undermining episcopal authority in Ireland,[71] Cullen again asked Higgins to use his best efforts to keep MacHale quiet. Higgins replied that Cullen knew how much he deplored public controversy, but that Murray had started it, and then went on to discuss the laying of the cornerstone of his new cathedral which could not be built for less than £50,000.[72] By this time, MacHale's deputy, Martin Loftus, had arrived in Rome, and since the archbishop was now no longer obliged to conduct his partisan business through a presumed neutral, Cullen decided to make his long deferred trip to Ireland, which he had not visited in some six years.

Before he left Rome, however, Cullen was asked by the Secretary of Propaganda, Monsignor Cadolini, to supply some information about the National System while on the spot in Ireland. Six weeks after his arrival in Ireland, Cullen reported to Cardinal Fransoni, the Prefect of Propaganda, "In the dioceses of Dublin and Kildare I have seen a good number of schools and I have noticed they could not be more Catholic than they are. The teachers are Catholic, the pupils are Catholic and the principal occupation of the children is learning the Christian doctrine."[73] "I do not think," he concluded, "there is any danger to the Faith." "Meanwhile," he added warily, "it is very necessary to proceed with great caution to bring about an end to this controversy." "To all appearances," Cullen reported to Monsignor Cadolini directly about a month later in a very long letter, "the system appears very satisfactory and for this reason it has quite a few defenders.[74] "Therefore," he warned, "it would seem that it would be very dangerous to condemn it as *undiquaque malum* [bad in every respect]." "The best and safest way to deal with the whole matter as I see it," he counseled, "would be allow things to remain as they are now even though in some schools there may be some abuse as a result of the nature of the teaching."

In Rome, meanwhile, the rival deputies Ennis and Loftus had presented their respective cases for and against the system to the propaganda in two long briefs.[75] Propaganda then turned the whole question over to a *"consultore"* for an impartial opinion. The consultor, Cornelius Van Everbroeck, a Dutch Jesuit, reviewed the case from beginning to end, and presented the propaganda with a 118-page opinion, which included a nine-page postscript.[76] At the end of his exhaustive consideration, Van Everbroeck concluded, that "the system is neither politively approved nor positively condemned, because in either case the most serious consequences are to be feared."[77]   This remarkable opinion, which advised, in effect, to leave things as they were, and attempt to secure all appropriate safeguards, was then abstracted in a brief, and amply buttressed up with suitable selections from Cullen's letters.[78]   The brief was then presented to the cardinals of propaganda, who were to make their decision at their monthly meeting, or *congregazione*, on December 22, 1840.[79]   The decision of the cardinals was promulgated in the form of a circular letter to the four archbishops of Ireland on January 16, 1841, under the signature of Cardinal Fransoni, the Prefect of Propaganda.[80] The sacred congregation has, the circular said, "resolved that no judgment should be definitely pronounced in this matter and that this kind of education should be left to the prudent discretion and religious conscience of each individual bishop, whereas its success must depend on the vigilant care of the pastors, on the various precautions to be adopted and on the future experience which time will supply."

V

At first, it might seem surprising, if not exasperating, that it should have taken Rome three years to decide to do nothing. To understand the mind of Rome, however, is to appreciate the fact that she prefers to govern by not making decisions.   What is perhaps even more surprising, and certainly more fundamental, is how Archbishop MacHale was able to raise and sustain so formidable a revolt in the face of the uncompromising position taken by Archbishop Murray and the bishops who supported him.   For over thirty years, Murray had been coadjutor and then Archbishop of Dublin.   His piety, zeal and learning were as much appreciated at Rome as they were in Ireland. Moreover, his arch-diocese alone, in terms of economic weight and political influence, counted for more than that of the Archbishop of Tuam, with the dioceses of his six suffragen bishops thrown in for good measure.

Most important of all, the need for money in the Irish Church was becoming ever more critical with each succeeding year. The population had been increasing at a frightening rate since the beginning of the century, and there was a consequent need to expand the Church establishment. At the same time, the resources on which the Church depended for its growth—mainly the Irish merchant class—were rapidly drying up. Caught between the decline of the merchant class and the awful poverty of an ever-increasing peasantry, the Irish Church simply could not afford to finance a primary-school system. Given the inescapable logic of the financial situation and the personal ascendency of Archbishop Murray, how did MacHale come so near to destroying the National System of Education?

The largest part of the answer to that question lies in the fact that Archbishop MacHale drew his main strength from the Irish theme which transcends all others—nationalism. For twenty years he had been a persistent and bitter public critic of British rule in Ireland, and had built up in the Irish mind the image of a patriot bishop. By 1840, the archbishop was, after Daniel O'Connell, the most popular man in Ireland. Add to this genuine popularity his unscrupulous behavior toward all who disagreed with him, and there emerges in MacHale a formidable type of demagogue whose influence and power are enhanced by his episcopal office, but are not entirely dependent on it. His simultaneous appeals, over the heads of his brother bishops, to the people in the public press and to Rome through Cullen, were less an indication of his conversion to either popular sovereignty or ultramontanism, than an accurate estimate by a very shrewd man as to where his power and influence were really rooted. Even the shrewdest men, however, are unable to anticipate all the variables, especially if one of the variables has been constant over a long period of time. The margin of defeat for MacHale, of course, was Cullen's crucial, though very discreet, defection after two and a half years service in the MacHale camp.

Archbishop MacHale's narrow nationalism, his unscrupulousness, even Cullen's discreet support, and even more discreet defection, are all the result of something wider and deeper in the history of the Irish Church. To understand their mentality is to realize the Church in Ireland has been living in a perpetual state of war since the Reformation. For centuries, therefore, the Irish Church has been on the defensive, and the tendency has been to react negatively rather than positively to the ways of the world. In the seventeenth century the Irish Church survived the assaults of a hostile English state. In the eighteenth century it weathered the attacks of a proselytizing Protestantism. In the ninteenth century it was hard-pressed by a revolutionary nationalism, and over the whole span, in company with all churches, it has had to combat an enervating secularism. This enormous pressure over a very long period of time has resulted in the Irish Church becoming reflexive before it was reflective, militant before it was tolerant, stern before it was gentle, and insular rather than cosmopolitan.

The quarrel initiated by Archbishop MacHale among the bishops in 1838 opened one of the most intense phases in this long war between the Irish Church and the British State. The tone and temper of the Irish Church, which had basked for some ten years in the warmth of Catholic emancipation, changed in 1838, and there began a clerical movement for power, which merged with, but was not submerged by the movement for repeal by Daniel O'Connell. A growing number of the younger bishops, led by MacHale, became more critical than ever of British rule in Ireland, but the majority were more timid, gratefully remembering the important changes that had come in their own day.

During the decade of the 1840's, as the older generation of bishops were either replaced by men more imbued with the new spirit, or were forced to a reconsideration of their position in the light of that spirit, the proportion of forward men grew until it finally became a pronounced majority. This change in temper and personnel of the Irish hierarchy was greatly accelerated by the kind of legislation brought forward by the British government. The policy of government in the Charitable Bequests Act, the increased grant to the Catholic seminary at Maynooth, the founding of the Queen's colleges, the introduction of a diplomatic relations bill with Rome, the proposal to pension the Irish clergy—were all more or less viewed by the majority of the bishops as attempts to divide the Irish Church from its people, and, as such, were fiercely resisted. A substantial minority, however, led by Archbishop Murray, were less suspicious, giving the government credit for good intentions, and supported all their proposed measures, except the pensioning of the clergy.

The Irish bishops fought these issues out in Ireland and at Rome with even greater fury and less scruple than they had disputed the education question. When the Great Famine, however, completely discredited British rule and those who supported it in Ireland, and Pius IX appointed Paul Cullen Archbishop of Armagh and Primate of All Ireland in 1849, the balance came down heavily on the side of the new men. They entered into their inheritance with joy, but they soon discovered their legacy was as dust and ashes. Ten years of general and civil war in the Irish Church had created an atmosphere which bred distrust, resulted in men becoming less fastidious about means to ends, loosened the bonds of clerical loyalty in the interests of advantage, and ended finally in emphasizing power at the expense of glory.

Notes

[1] Cullen Papers, March 10, 1838. The Cullen Papers referred to in this article are located in the Irish College, Rome, and are hereafter designated CP.

[2] *Dublin Evening Post,* February 13, 1838.

[3] *Ibid.,* February 24, 1938.

[4] CP, February 24, 1838.

[5] CP, April 19, 1838.

[6] *Ibid.*

[7] CP, April 28, 1838.

[8] CP, June 13, 1838.

[9] CP, July 3, 1838.

[10] CP, July 28, 1838.

[11] CP, August 6, 1838 (copy).

[12] CP, August 26, 1838 (Quoting Murray's of August 22, 1838).

[13] *Ibid.*

[14] *Dublin Evening Post,* October 23, 1838. Murray's letter is dated October 22, 1838.

[15] *Ibid.,* November 3, 1838. MacHale's letter is dated Feast of the Apostles SS. Simon and Jude.

[16] *Ibid.,* November 10, 1838. Murray's letter is dated November 8, 1838.

[17] *Ibid.,* November 24, 1838. MacHale's letter is dated Feast of the Redemption, 1838.

[18] CP, December 12, 1838.

[19] CP, January 4, 1839.

[20] CP, December 24, 1838.

[21] CP, January 3, 1839.

[22] CP, January 23, 1839.

[23] CP, January 3, 1839.

24 CP, January 30, 1839.

25 CP, February 1, 1839.

26 *Ibid.*

27 CP, August 22, 1839.

28 CP, January 28, 1839.

29 CP, February 4, 1839.

30 *Ibid.*

31 *Ibid.*

32 CP, February 1, 1839.

33 CP, February 1, 1839.

34 CP, March 13, 1839.

35 CP, April 20, 1839.

36 CP, May 15, 1839.

37 CP, March 26, 1839. See also CP, April 8, 1839, MacHale to Cullen. "It is extraordinary how men otherwise so enlightened would suffer themselves to be led astray by misrepresentations so silly and malevolent. We are determined not to suffer the political agents of the government to grasp the concerns of our religion. Therefore these agents represent us as interfering in politics! We really do and will interfere so far as to defect their wily political machinations. This is the sum total of our interference and if we do not persevere a sort of political papacy claiming complete jurisdiction over our Ecclesiastical affairs without reference to Rome will be established in Ireland."

38 CP, March 26, 1839.

39 CP, April 14, 1839.

40 CP, May 2, 1839.

41 CP, July 12, 1839.

42 *Ibid.,* "The Bigots would not fail to avail themselves of this occasion to brand us as Patrons of ignorance under the tyrannical influence of a foreign power; and the very poor themselves, who find by experience the minds of their children opening under this System to useful knowledge with perfect safety to their religious principles, would undoubtedly look with much less reverence than heretofore on the decisions of Rome. In fact it is doubtful if even the Holy See itself could succeed against the clear convictions of the people."

43 CP, August 22, 1839.

44 CP, October 28, 1839.

45 CP, November 4, 1839.

46 CP, November 28, 1839.

47 CP, December 6, 1839.

48 CP, December 6, 1839.

49 *Ibid.*

50 CP, December 13, 1839. Higgins suggested that the Pope should write each bishop a private letter "giving the opinions of the Holy See on the controversy, and instructing the bishop at once to adopt them, at the same time causing us to be publicly addressed from Rome *as a body,* and declining to take the case out of our own hands. We might then in full assembly come to resolutions agreeing perfectly with the Pope's confidential orders."

51 CP, December 13, 1839.

52 CP, December 21, 1839.

53 CP, December 13, 1839.
54 CP, January 17, 1840.
55 CP, January 18, 1840.
56 CP, January 18, 1840.
57 CP, January 28, 1840.
58 CP, September 17, 1839.
59 CP, November 28, 1839.
60 CP, January 28, 1840.
61 CP, February 14, 1840. This date is obviously incorrect in the text.
62 *Ibid.*
63 CP, February 14, 1840.
64 CP, February 22, 1840.
65 CP, February 24, 1840.
66 *Ibid.*, See *Freeman's Journal*, February 11, 1840.
67 CP, February 28, 1840.
68 *Dublin Evening Post*, March 10, 1840. MacHale's letter is dated March 1, 1840.
69 *Ibid.*, April 25, 1840. See "To the Archbishop of Tuam" from "A Priest of the United Dioceses of Kildare and Leighlin," dated April 23, 1840, for a most reasonable attempt to come to terms with issues.
70 *Ibid.*, March 31, 1840. See letter of Rev. T. O'Malley to MacHale, dated London, March 27, 1840, as the best example of the "Rough and Tumble."
71 CP, April 4, 1840.
72 CP, May 4, 1840.
73 Archives of the Propaganda Fide, Rome. *Scritture Riferite Nei Congressi*, vol. 27 (1839-42), ff. 274-275. Cullen to Fransoni, Ballitore, August 7, 1840. This letter is reprinted and translated into English in Rev. Peader MacSuibhne, *Paul Cullen and his Contemporaries* (1961), I, 229-230.
74 *Ibid.*, ff. 270-271. Cullen to Cadolini, Dublin, September 13, 1840. For translation see MacSuibhne, pp. 231-235.
75 *Ibid.*, ff. 386-401. Giovanni Ennis, "Memoria intorno allo stato dell educatione de' poveri in Irlanda." No Date. See ff. 282-339 for Martin Loftus, to Pope, September 12, 1840.
76 Archives of the Propaganda Fide, Rome. *Acta*, vol. 203, ff. 419-79. "Systema nec positive damnandum esse, quia in utroque casu gravissimae sequelae timendae essent."
77 *Ibid.*, f. 472.
78 *Ibid.*, ff. 410-11.
79 *Ibid.*, f. 412.
80 Scritture, f. 427. "Circolare del Enmo Prefetto di Propaganda al Quattro Arcivescovi d'Irlanda sull' insegnamento nazionali."

Comment

Gilbert A. Cahill

Because of rather extensive research I have done in Irish and English newspapers, in the periodical press and pamphlets, in parliamentary committee reports on various aspects of the Irish question, and in Hansard's parliamentary debates, I would recommend certain modifications in Emmet Larkin's essay, particularly Part V, which relates his study to broader currents in Irish history.

In several places Larkin speaks of the importance of public opinion. In his concluding remarks he indicates the significance of nationalism as a force in the evolving Irish historical process. Several times he speaks of a "war mentality," and at one point relates it to the Catholic Emancipation Act. Paradoxically, Catholic emancipation did little to mitigate the "war mentality" in Ireland or England. In fact, a strong case can be made for the opposite view, that Catholic emancipation enlarged the area of tension so that the "war mentality" applied not only to Archbishop MacHale and Southern Ireland but to Northern Ireland, Scotland, and England as well. Carried from above, its passage, as J. H. Hexter has aptly observed, was accompanied by no revolution in cultural, religious, or national attitudes.[1] Carried by the wrong man for the wrong reasons, Catholic emancipation was legislated without the provisions that might have given the English State some control over the Irish hierarchy, was accompanied by limitation of the suffrage in Ireland in 1829, and followed by an Irish coercion bill in 1833 and O'Connell's demand for repeal of the Union in 1834.[2] From 1834 Catholic emancipation was thought a mistake and was directly associated in the Irish Protestant, Scotch, and English public minds with repeal of the Union. A revisionist movement to repeal Catholic emancipation was sponsored by the ultra-Tories, with considerable support from the English and northern Irish press. The vote of the House of Commons in 1834 and 1848 on repeal of the Union faithfully mirrored the opinion of the nation, and public opinion, if anything, was even more nativistic and nationalistic than the vote in Parliament indicated.[3]

The initiative in unleashing the Protestant side of this nativistic "war mentality" was taken by Irish members of the House of Lords in 1834. Their objective was to export the garrison psychology of Protestant Ireland to England and Scotland. Their base of operations in that year was the six counties of the north; their technique was the public meeting; their operation was directed by an executive committee organized as the Dublin Conservative Society; their message and ideological bias was spread by the newspaper and periodical press.[4]   What was accomplished in northern Ireland in 1834 was successfully carried to England and Scotland in 1835 and 1836.   Once again the technique was the public meeting, principally but not necessarily in the large English and Scottish cities with large Irish populations. The operation was directed by the Dublin Conservative Society and was supported by a majority of the lords temporal and spiritual in the House of Lords and the ultra-Tories in Commons.   The institutions securing public support were the Orange Society, Exeter Hall, and the Protestant Association. The message was carried by a section of the periodical press and a powerful combination of English daily newspapers, including the *Times, Morning Herald, Morning Post* and *Standard.* The campaign, which assumed the dimensions of a Protestant crusade, was continued in 1837, 1838, 1839, 1840, and 1841; in 1841 the Melbourne government was defeated by a majority of eleven, in a packed house on Lord Morpeth's registration bill.[5]

Through the years 1834-38 Exeter Hall, the Protestant Association, and a substantial section of the English press contended that O'Connell's objective, when he was supporting the Whigs in Commons, was the repeal of the Union.   In addition, from 1834-41, a number of Irish questions were perennially debated in both Lords and Commons.   These measures included the payment of tithes, the Irish Church (especially the famous appropriation clause pertaining to education in the 1834 and 1835 bills), the Irish municipal corporation act, the Irish registration act, and Irish outrages.   These issues were discussed at great length in the press, at public meetings, and in Parliament.   Though these issues were not religious, they were discussed as such, and were also connected to O'Connell's goal, the repeal of the Union.[6]   This repetitious debate was part of the Protestant crusade; its content was an anti-Irish and anti-Catholic xenophobia which was constantly related to the political and religious stereotype of

"Popery." The 1830-40 version of this centuries-old English historical stereotype was the existence of a conspiracy on the part of the Irish hierarchy and priesthood to subvert the British constitution. The plot was conceived by the Irish hierarchy and perpetuated through the theological preparation of priests at the Roman Catholic Seminary at Maynooth.[7] The key to the plot was the theology textbook used at Maynooth—Peter Dens's theology—and particularly with Dens's definition of a public oath. The Irish hierarchy's definition of an oath written into law by the Catholic Emancipation Act made a mockery of the guarantees against subversion of the British constitution.

While, according to Larkin, the quarrel among the Irish hierarchy on the National System of Education did not break into the open until 1838-41, the education issue was a continuing one from 1834-41 between, on the one hand, the lords temporal and spiritual, the Orange Society, the Protestant Association, Exeter Hall, the Kildare-Place Society, other voluntary associations, and a large section of the press (both Irish and English), and on the other, the Irish hierarchy and O'Connell. To understand the "war mentality" of 1838, then, it is necessary to see it in a larger dialectal complex than a conflict between two factions of the Irish hierarchy; to relate the education issue to the several other issues debated in and out of Parliament and to the anti-Irish and anti-Catholic nativism which accompanied this "no-Popery" campaign; and to trace the development of the education issue from 1834-38 in the evolving Protestant crusade.

By 1834 there was an observable groundswell against the National School System of Education in Ireland. Several public meetings were held in England under the auspices of certain lords spiritual. The meetings were addressed by the Rev. Mortimer O'Sullivan, an active participant of the Dublin Conservative Society, and the Rev. James Graham, a chaplain of the Orange Society and secretary of the Kildare-Place Society.[9] As a result of these meetings, petitions were sent to Commons which emphasized the Church-in-danger theme, thereby connecting the education issue to the Irish Church and tithe issues. Throughout 1835, 1836, and 1837 the Revs. Mortimer O'Sullivan and Robert McGhee, Irish Evangelicals, and the Rev. Henry Cooke, an influential northern Irish Presbyterian, toured England and Scotland under the auspices of Exeter Hall and the Protestant Association. Their meetings were well attended and the leading English and Irish newspapers carried accounts of their addresses, which sometimes ran from twelve to thirteen full columns. These fiery "Biblicals" mounted a "no-Popery" attack against the Irish hierarchy, particularly Archbishops Murray and MacHale, and O'Connell. The contents of the textbooks of Peter Dens, used at Maynooth, were endlessly examined as proof of a Popish plot. And as Archbishop Murray wrote to Lord Melbourne in a letter published in most English and Irish newspapers, the purpose of the Evangelical attack on him was to discredit both the national board, of which Murray was a member, and the National System of Education in Ireland.[10]

Archbishop Murray on several occasions thereafter wrote to the English and Irish newspapers. His letters, however, were always rational and even-tempered, and as far as possible, he refused to enter into religious-political controversy. This was not the case with Archbishop MacHale, who was a prolific letter writer to both English and Irish newspapers. The tone he adopted was that of religious nationalism, and as he got caught up in the polemics of religious and nationalistic controversy, he became the scapegoat of the anti-Irish and anti-Catholic English press, and particularly of Exeter Hall and the Protestant Association.[11] Certain members of the Association did an effective job of keeping the controversy alive. The Protestant Association, for example, established the Achill mission in MacHale's diocese where its pastor actively carried on the job of proselytism and where alleged attacks upon the mission supplied the Rev. Edward Nangle with materials for continuous criticism of Archbishop MacHale for the lack of religious toleration in his diocese. The simple theme was that there could be religious toleration of Roman Catholics in Britain because there they were protected by law. In Ireland, there was only persecution of Protestants, because in Ireland there was no observance of law, especially in the south.[12] This theme blended nicely with the larger problem of Irish outrages investigated by a House of Lords committee in 1839. The tempo of this anti-Irish, anti-Catholic, anti-MacHale and anti-O'Connell attack accelerated between 1838 and 1841. Its bias won victories for the Conservatives in a number of English by-elections and helped to give that party a majority in the House of Commons by 1841.[13] From 1838-41 the national board and National System of Education in Ireland were associated in the English and Irish mind with Lord Brougham's proposal for the reform and extension of secular education in England.[14]

This larger ideological conflict must be kept in mind when the historian appraises the motives and actions of Archbishop Mac-Hale. By 1838 he was deep involved in a national conflict which transcended that with Archbishop Murray. The counterpart of MacHale's "war mentality" is to be found in the activities of the "Biblicals" and Evangelicals of the 1831's, in the letters and speeches of the Rev. O'Sullivan, Rev. McGhee and Rev. Mc-Neile, who were most active and most effective. These men advocated the extinction of Catholicism in Ireland, and they were answered in like manner by MacHale. The key, then, to much of the archbishop's behavior is to be found not so much in terms of the economic factor as in this nativistic context.

Notes

[1] J. H. Hexter, "The Protestant Revival and the Catholic Question in England 1778-1829," *Journal of Modern History*, VIII (1936), 297-318.

[2] According to J. P. Meyer, editor of Alexis de Tocqueville's *Journeys to England and Ireland* (London: Faber and Faber, 1957), p. 125, when in 1834 O'Connell brought the question of repeal before the House of Commons, "he gained the vote of only one English member."

[3] This campaign can be followed in the pages of the *Dublin Evening Mail* throughout 1834, particularly from August to December.

[4] Elie Halévy, *The Triumph of Reform, 1830-1841* (New York: Barnes and Noble, 1961), p. 342.

[5] For the campaign of the Protestant Association in 1836 against the Irish Church Bill and the Irish Municipal Corporations Bill, cf. the reports on their meetings in the following issues of the *Times*, May 12, July 15, 21, 27, 30, August 3, 18, September 20, October 15, November 10, 28, 1836.

[6] *Ibid.*, June 15, 22, July 10, 11, 1835—"Maynooth"; July 6, 7, 10, 13, 14, 16, 17, 18, 1835—"Dens' Theology"; November 4, 5, 6, 7, 9, 10, 12, 18, 1835—"Popery."

[7] Gilbert A. Cahill, "Irish Catholicism and English Toryism," *Review of Politics*, XIX (January, 1957), 62-77.

[8] *Dublin Evening Mail*, November 7, 1834. The *Mail* carried an address of the Reverend James Graham at Cheltenham of the Friends of the Kildare-Place Society. Also *Dublin Evening Mail*, January 22, 1834, ". . . One word more, and we have done. Can our rulers be unaware of the fact—and fact we reassure them it is—that the great majority of meetings for Repeal of the Union, and the propagation of sedition, have been held in the 'school houses' under the protection and patronage of the new Board of Education."

9 *Dublin Evening Mail,* July 3, 1835: editorial on Archbishop Murray's letter to Lord Melbourne; *Courier,* July 4, 1835: editorial on Murray's letter; *Globe,* July 17, 1835.

10 *Standard,* September 16, 1835: editorial on letter from Doctor Murray on Peter Dens's theology. October 13, 14, 15, 1835: cf. Doctor Murray's Letter to the Protestants of Great Britain and the *Standard's* editorials on same.

11 *Warder,* March 8, 1834; *Standard,* October 14, 1835; *Courier,* October 29, 1835.

12 The *Times,* December 29, 1835, "The Protestant Association—The Achill Mission."

13 Cahill, "Irish Catholicism," p. 70.

14 Amy Margaret Gilbert, *The Work of Lord Brougham for Education in England* (Chambersburg, Pa., 1922), pp. 100-1.

A Note on Contributors

JOHN J. APPEL teaches at Michigan State University, specializing in social and intellectual history. His publications include "The New England Origins of the American Irish Historical Society" (*New England Quarterly*, Dec. 1960) and "Betzemer: A Cognomen for the Irish" (*American Speech*, Dec. 1963).

MAURICE BEEBE, professor of English at Purdue University, is the editor of *Modern Fiction Studies*. In addition to editing three volumes of criticism, he has published numerous essays on a variety of subjects. His most recent book is *Ivory Towers and Sacred Founts: The Artist as Hero in Fiction from Goethe to Joyce*.

EDWARD BRANDABUR, assistant professor of English at the University of Illinois, has contributed to the *Journal of English and Germanic Philology*. He has completed a book on *Dubliners* and is presently at work on one about *Ulysses*, in addition to studies of Eliot and Yeats.

RAY B. BROWNE, associate professor of English at Purdue University, is the author of thirty articles in various magazines as well as the editor of seven books in print or in press. He is currently working on a critical study of Melville.

GILBERT A. CAHILL, professor of European history at the State University College at Cortland, New York, is a former president of the New York State Association of European Historians and president of the American Committee for Irish studies. He has published papers in various quarterlies. He is now editing "The Great Reform Bill of 1832—Liberal or Conservative?" for D. C. Heath's *Problems in European Civilization* and is at work on a book, *The Irish Protestant Party, Papaphobia and English Nativism 1825-1848*.

MAURICE HARMON, a native of Ireland, is currently teaching Irish literature at the University of Notre Dame. He has published articles in Irish, English, and American journals, and is currently working on a study of Sean O'Faolain.

REV. JEREMIAH C. LEHANE, a native of Blarney, County Cork, Ireland, is chairman of the English Department of De Paul University, Chicago. He is book critic for the *Chicago New World* and *Chicago Tribune*.

EMMET LARKIN, assistant professor of history in the Humanities Department at the Massachusetts Institute of Technology, is writing a history of the Roman Catholic Church in Ireland in the nineteenth century. He is also the author of the new biography, *James Larkin, 1876-1947: Irish Labour Leader*.

MACEDWARD LEACH, professor of English and folklore at the University of Pennsylvania, has been president and secretary-treasurer of the American Folklore Society. The author of many articles and reviews, he has edited Middle English texts, notably *Amis and Amiloon* (1937) and *Paris and Vienne* (1957), as well as *The Ballad Book* and, with Tristram P. Coffin, *The Critics and the Ballad.*

RICHARD J. LOFTUS, assistant professor of English at the University of Illinois, is the author of *Nationalism in Modern Anglo-Irish Poetry.*

VIVIAN MERCIER, associate professor of English, City University, New York, was born in Dublin. He is the author of *The Irish Comic Tradition,* co-editor of *1000 Years of Irish Prose,* and editor of *Great Irish Short Stories.*

WILLIAM J. ROSCELLI, assistant professor of English at Purdue, is an associate editor of *The Journal of Reading* and has published articles on Shakespeare, Milton, and Swift. He is currently writing a book on Milton's *Adam* and is compiling an annotated bibliography of Robert Louis Stevenson.

GEORGE BRANDON SAUL, professor of English at the University of Connecticut, has published several hundred poems, articles, and reviews, as well as sixteen books and chapbooks, including the *Prolegomena* relating to Yeats. His next book will be the edited *Age of Yeats: Irish Literature.*

74
35
76
77
79
83
85